Coach Hall

COACH HALL

My Life On and Off the Court

Joe B. Hall
with Marianne Walker

Foreword by Rick Bozich

UNIVERSITY PRESS OF KENTUCKY

Published by The University Press of Kentucky

Scholarly publisher for the Commonwealth,
serving Bellarmine University, Berea College, Centre
College of Kentucky, Eastern Kentucky University,
The Filson Historical Society, Georgetown College,
Kentucky Historical Society, Kentucky State University,
Morehead State University, Murray State University,
Northern Kentucky University, Transylvania University,
University of Kentucky, University of Louisville,
and Western Kentucky University.
All rights reserved.

Editorial and Sales Offices: The University Press of Kentucky
663 South Limestone Street, Lexington, Kentucky 40508–4008
www.kentuckypress.com

Unless otherwise noted, photos are from the author's collection.

Library of Congress Cataloging-in-Publication Data

Names: Hall, Joe B. (Joe Beasman), author. | University Press of Kentucky.
Title: Coach Hall : my life on and off the court / Joe B. Hall, with Marianne
    Walker ; foreword by Rick Bozich.
Description: Lexington : University Press of Kentucky, 2019. | Includes
    bibliographical references and index.
Identifiers: LCCN 2019025432 | ISBN 9780813178561 (Hardcover) | ISBN
    9780813178592 (ePub) | ISBN 9780813178585 (PDF)
Subjects: LCSH: Hall, Joe B. (Joe Beasman) | Basketball coaches—United
    States—Biography. | University of Kentucky—Basketball.
Classification: LCC GV884.H23 H35 2019 | DDC 796.323092 [B] —dc23

Member of the Association
of University Presses

*For my family and for all the players
and assistant coaches on all my teams*

Contents

Photos follow page 90

Foreword

Some basketball truths last forever. Don't give up the baseline. Keep your eye on the rim. Always look for the open man.

And never be the man who follows The Man.

Let somebody else take that job. Then you follow that guy because chances are he'll be pushed out the door before you know it.

Ask the folks at UCLA, who are still looking for somebody who makes them as satisfied as the Bruins were with the incomparable John Wooden. Gene Bartow lasted two seasons as Wooden's first replacement. Ditto for Gary Cunningham and Larry Brown, the next two guys who volunteered for the assignment.

Ask the folks at North Carolina, who cycled through Bill Guthridge (three seasons) and Matt Doherty (three seasons) before settling on Roy Williams as the guy capable of replacing Dean Smith.

Indiana is a similar story. Archie Miller is the fifth coach trying to make IU fans move past Bob Knight.

Never be the man who follows The Man. Remember that advice.

Then remember to express more admiration for Joe B. Hall, a genuine Kentucky icon, the guy Marianne Walker has captured so completely in this book. Joe B. Hall was not only the man who followed The Man (Adolph Rupp); Hall was a man who did the job remarkably well.

Try to imagine the circumstances when Hall took over the iconic Kentucky program in 1972. He replaced Rupp, who won 876 games, once the NCAA Division I record. Four of those Rupp victories came in NCAA championship games, an achievement exceeded only by Wooden.

Joe B. Hall replaced a Hall of Fame coach whose name was revered for basketball greatness from Paintsville to Paducah as well as from New York City to Los Angeles. Adolph Rupp *was* Kentucky basketball, the guy who built the brand with Ralph Beard, Cliff Hagan, Frank Ramsey, Dan Issel, and others who made Memorial Coliseum crackle with energy.

Joe B. Hall replaced that coach and did it well in an occasionally uncomfortable atmosphere because Rupp was not ready to give up his job. The former coach, forced reluctantly to the sidelines because of his age, watched every move that Hall made.

The world knew this because Rupp spoke about his displeasure to anybody who asked. The world knew this if it watched any television during the first season of Rupp's retirement because he continued to host a television show that was just as popular as Hall's TV show.

While Bartow bailed as Wooden's replacement at UCLA after two seasons, Guthridge stepped down at North Carolina as Smith's replacement after three seasons, and Mike Davis was fired at Indiana as Knight's successor after six seasons, Hall delivered at Kentucky for thirteen solid seasons. Hall stayed and succeeded over a longer stretch than those three guys combined. That's impressive.

He delivered an NCAA championship in 1978. It is remembered as UK's fifth NCAA title, but it was the school's first national title in the fiercely competitive world of integrated college basketball. Rupp was a master, but Hall did a masterful job maintaining Kentucky's dominance in the Southeastern Conference, which finally started taking basketball seriously by adding coaches like C. M. Newton, Hugh Durham, and Norm Sloan as well as dazzling players like Dominique Wilkins, Charles Barkley, and Bernard King. Keeping Kentucky on top was not guaranteed, but on top is where the Wildcats remained because of Hall.

If you need numbers to make your case for the great work Hall did, there are plenty to cite. There was the 1978 NCAA title. There was the 1975 Final Four appearance that included a regional final victory over an unbeaten Indiana team. There was another trip to the Final Four in 1984.

In thirteen seasons, Hall won 297 games, with a victory percentage of nearly 75 percent. Four times he was honored as the SEC Coach of the Year. His teams won at least a part of eight SEC titles—and remember, the SEC was packed with talented players during that stretch.

Credit Hall with being one of the first coaches who understood the benefits of strength training and year-round conditioning. It's standard operating procedure today, but it wasn't in 1973. Hall changed that—and the game. Hall brought a sophisticated training program to UK basketball. When other coaches rolled their eyes at the extra lifting and running that Hall demanded and also worried that the coach was turning his players into brutes, the coach winked. He wanted to be certain he had a fresher, stronger team in March—and usually, he did.

There's more. If Rupp recruited the first African American player to Kentucky, it was Hall who successfully integrated the UK program, a development that the legendary Cawood Ledford recognized as important. Hall welcomed Merion Haskins, Larry Johnson, Jack Givens, James Lee, Dwane Casey, Truman Claytor, Sam Bowie, Derrick Hord, Charles Hurt, Dirk Minniefield, Melvin Turpin, and many others into the program. Players within the state had a home in Lexington.

He hired Leonard Hamilton, the program's first African American assistant coach, more than two decades before C. M. Newton hired Tubby Smith as Kentucky's first African American head coach.

Hall was there to shake Smith's hand when Smith took control of the program he loved so much, just as Hall was always there to support Eddie Sutton, Rick Pitino, Billy Gillispie, and John Calipari, the other coaches who followed him. Hall observed. He cheered. He did not second-guess.

Over the last three decades, no sight in Rupp Arena has been more comforting than that of Hall cheering for the Wildcats from his trademark seat several rows off the floor across from the visitors' bench. People loved the entertaining radio show he hosted with former Louisville coach Denny Crum. They appreciated him for the way that he was always there for Kentucky. Former players, opposing coaches, broadcasters, writers, and fans made their way to Hall's seat to thank him for his service to the program as well as the university.

You can't fake being a gentleman for more than thirty years. Hall didn't have to fake anything. He was eager to shake a hand, pose for a picture, answer a question, or offer an encouraging word. That has always been Joe.

I always admired Hall for more than his coaching victories. I admired him for all the changes he brought to Kentucky basketball— and for proving you can be the man who follows The Man, and do it with kindness, humility, and grace.

The Joe B. Hall story is more than a wonderful narrative—it's an important tale and one that Marianne Walker tells so well.

Rick Bozich
WDRB Sports

Prologue

Kevin Grevey's Awakening

On one occasion before one of our ball games, the band—as it always does before games—was playing "My Old Kentucky Home." Everyone in the stadium was standing and singing along with the band leader. All of the players were standing at attention and singing too, except one—freshman Kevin Grevey. Something had struck him funny; he was laughing and whispering to the boys next to him. He was a distraction. Right before the start of the game, while we were in the dressing room, I explained to him why his behavior was not acceptable. "That song is our state song," I said, "and it is important to all Kentuckians." By not paying attention while it was sung, he was being disrespectful to the song and to all of us. Kevin, who was from Hamilton, Ohio, said he didn't know anything about the song. I told him to learn! I wanted him to sing all the words to me at practice on Monday. And he did.

Weeks later, returning from an afternoon game in Florida, we were flying over Tennessee as darkness began to fall. I asked Dick Parsons, my assistant, to ask Kevin to come sit next to me. I told Kevin to look out the window and tell me what he saw. He leaned over and looked out the window and then turned back to me, puzzled. "Why, everything is dark, Coach." I told him to wait just a few minutes and look out again and tell me what he saw, for by then we would be flying over Kentucky. He was surprised as he looked out: "Why, there are lights on everywhere now—even out in the farming areas."

Then I said to Kevin, "Now do you see the difference between Tennessee and Kentucky at near midnight during basketball season? Those homes where the lights are on are the homes of your fans, the homes of those who support all of us here on this plane. Those people are staying up late at night watching our games on delayed television. Those lights tell you how important basketball is to Kentuckians. These people hold you and your teammates in high regard. Without this great number of people supporting us, we are nothing, Kevin. Their support is essential to our success. This is why it is so important for you to understand why you must respect our state song, and all these people who back you and your teammates. You owe these fans respect. Don't you ever forget that."

1

Why "Joe B. Hall"?

I should not talk so much about myself if there were anybody
else I knew as well.

Henry David Thoreau

Until I was nine or ten, everyone called me Joe or Joe Hall.
Then one day my grandmother Laura Harney, for reasons
known only to her, pulled me aside and told me my name was "too
short and too plain." She said, "Let's add your middle initial to make
it more interesting. From now on, you say your name is Joe B., not
just Joe. It's Joe B. Hall." This is what she told me about the B.

I was born in Cynthiana, Kentucky, on November 30, 1928,
and in those days, doctors came to the house to deliver babies. Dr.
MacDowell delivered me at our home. Before he left that wintry
day, he wanted to complete my birth certificate, but my parents
had not decided on my name. The doctor told my mother, "I'll
stop by tomorrow to check on you and the baby and get his
name then." But by the next day, my parents still had not chosen
a name. Tired of waiting for a couple who had had nine months
to choose their baby's name and then still couldn't decide, the
doctor went ahead and named me himself—after a man whom my
parents had never met. It was a man he respected and admired—
Joe Beasman, the first legislator in state government elected from
our area, Harrison County. The middle initial in my name stands
for Beasman, not basketball, as I have often told people. I never
met Mr. Beasman, although I often wish I had.

My hometown lies on the banks of the South Licking River
in Harrison County. It is twenty-eight miles north of Lexington,

1

where I have spent nearly all my adult life. Cynthiana has an interesting history. During the Civil War, General John Hunt Morgan and his Confederate Calvary regiment fought two battles there. In trying to run the Yankees off, they burned a stable, starting a horrific fire that destroyed most of downtown in 1862. Some famous people are part of Cynthiana's history: Henry Clay, William Jennings Bryan, Governor Joseph Desha, and John Phillips Sousa, the composer and band leader, just to name a few. Cynthiana has named a bridge and a street after me and had an artist paint a mural of me on a building downtown. My deceased parents, relatives, and friends would have gotten a kick out of knowing that kind of honor had been bestowed on me.

During the 1930s and '40s when I was growing up, Cynthiana had about four thousand residents, and life was lived at a much slower pace than it is now. Nearly everybody knew everybody else, everybody's children, and everybody's business. No such official state office called "Child Services" existed in those days—most people just looked out for one another's kids. If some kid did something he ought not have, his dad or mom would know about it before that kid got home. If an adult corrected someone else's kid for wrongdoing, it was appreciated, not considered interfering.

Billy, my older brother whom I adored, and I played in the streets, swam, hunted, fished, and roamed all over town. We helped ourselves to fruit off neighbor's trees and strawberries out of their gardens. Nobody ever ran us off. Our car keys were left in the car overnight, and doors to our home were never locked. Our needs and pleasures were simple ones. We had none of the electronics that kids have today to distract us (thank goodness). The highlight of many of our summers was camping with Mom and Dad at Licking River. Other families would go with us, so we had lots of children to play with. During the weekdays, our parents would leave us in the care of another adult while they went into town to work. When they returned in the late afternoon, we would have a big cookout. Those were happy times.

My parents were devout members of the Cynthiana Christian Church and raised us children to be the same. I still am a member of the Christian Church, but I have always been ecumenical and have friends in all faiths. Growing up, I attended Sunday school classes at the Baptist church because Bill Boswell, my football coach, someone I liked and respected, taught those classes. Until my voice changed, I sang in the Episcopalian boys' soprano choir.

The values I learned when I was young are the same ones that I have carried with me throughout my life, and they have served me well. I have taught them to my own children and to the boys I coached.

2

Hard Times

Cultivate the habit of being grateful for every good thing that comes to you, and to give thanks continuously, and because all things have contributed to your advancement, you include all things in your gratitude.

Ralph Waldo Emerson

I grew up during the height of the Great Depression when times were especially hard and across the nation nearly everyone's motto was "Make do or do without." My brother Billy was three and half years older than I, and my sister Laura Jane nine years younger. By the time she was born the economy had improved, and my parents were financially better off. It was not until we were much older that Billy and I learned how truly difficult things had been during the early 1930s. As little boys, we were happy, playing outdoors, inventing things to do. Our needs were simple: fishing poles, bait, basketball, and bikes.

My parents are Ruth Harney and Charles Curtis Hall. For the first six years of my life, my mother was a stay-at-home mom. My dad worked as a mechanic or a welder when those jobs were available in Cynthiana. He could do just about anything, though, and he did a little bit of everything to support his family. Although he worked hard every chance he had, he still had trouble finding enough work to enable him to support us the way he wanted to.

Dad was my hero. I thought he could do anything—and he could. My grandmother told me that when Dad was a little boy there was a newspaper cartoon featuring a kid named Bill. When Dad started hanging around the garage shop where the guys were repairing cars, they started calling him Bill (after the cartoon character) and that name stuck. He grew up known as Bill, not Charles. The guys would let him do little jobs on the cars, not for pay but to learn. Later he became a good mechanic, but he did not stay in that field long. He learned to master other trades, including building and plumbing. He never fooled with electrical work, though. But he could rehaul an engine and fix anything wrong with a car. He could remodel a car to look like it had never been wrecked.

My father's mother died very young, and his maternal grandmother, Missouri Bullock, raised him to be a firm believer in God, family, hard work, fair play, and discipline of mind and body. My father taught us the same values. He saw to it that we had a well-rounded education, both secular and religious. He wanted us to learn how to take care of ourselves in any situation, to get ahead in life, and he always wanted us to stay close to the family. He and Mom expected us to be good people, to grow up to be respected members of our community, wherever that was. As parents, they took care of all our needs—but very few of our wants. They taught us to work for what we wanted and to manage and take care of what we had. They let us do all the outdoors things we wanted to do and play all kinds of sports. We didn't hear "No" often, or "Don't go there or don't do that; you might get hurt." They let us learn some things by making mistakes.

After barely getting through the crisis of the early 1930s, my parents decided to move to Florida where they had heard there were job opportunities. In the early summer of 1934, when the world's economy bottomed out, they tied a tent on the roof of our car and packed all our necessary belongings and crammed them into our four-door Dodge. Before dawn one morning, they woke Billy and me and told us to get in the car—we were leaving for Florida. In those days, cars were large and roomy, but they had no seatbelts, air-conditioning, or radios (as least ours didn't have a radio), and gas cost a dime a gallon.

That first night, we stopped somewhere in Georgia. Dad pitched the tent in a field near the road, and we spent the night there. We got up the next day, folded the tent, and moved on to a trailer park in Miami. That next morning, Dad went to the main office of the Miami Laundry Service and asked if there were any job openings. He was told no, that there were ten applicants already for every job in the plant. My dad persisted, though, asking if any of their salesmen were on vacation; when the guy said yes, there was one, Dad pleaded, "Let me run his route while he is gone, and if I don't double his work, you don't have to pay me, but if I do, you give me a job." Dad did double that man's route, and he got a job. He soon became head of the spotting department in the clothes-cleaning business. It was then he learned a trade that helped him later.

My mother soon found work too, helping a lady who owned a florist shop. Although Mom had no experience working with flowers, she learned quickly and enjoyed her job. Later she owned her own florist business.

When we arrived in Florida early that summer in 1934, Billy was ten and I was six. The weather was beautiful. Being outdoors there was different from our experiences in Cynthiana. Standing on the beach, there was nothing but blue sky, water, and sand for as far as we could see. Life in Florida was good for us. We lived in a small rented house, close to an elementary school, on the beach. From our house, we watched the first hotel go up on the beach: the Jack Dempsey.

3

The Epiphany

A disciplined mind leads to happiness, and an undisciplined mind leads to suffering.

Dalai Lama XIV

Not knowing anyone in Miami yet and without Grandma there to look after us, our parents had no choice but to leave Billy and me unattended, to trust us to behave ourselves while they worked. I don't remember any instructions they gave us, but I am certain they left some. Today, leaving two little boys alone among strangers all day in an unfamiliar city does not sound like a good idea at all, but they had no alternative. Back then, times were different, and the world was in some ways safer.

By the time Billy and I woke up in the mornings, our parents had already left for work. They would always leave enough change on the table for each of us to buy our lunch. However, we dined on snacks and soda pops instead. Billy and I slept late every morning and then headed straight for the beach to roll in the sand, build castles, and swim in the ocean. We swam much farther than my parents, no doubt, ever thought we would. We felt as if the ocean was ours, and we were not afraid of anything. We swam clear out past the sandbars, we swam across canals full of barracudas and other dangerous fish, and we learned to knife through big waves without getting squashed. We saw no dangers in anything we did. Our parents had not warned us of any dangers, I guess because they never even thought we would do some of the things we did. At an early age, then, we got very comfortable in the ocean—and I mean way out in the ocean. The beach was not crowded then. Usually no one paid any attention to us, although occasionally a lifeguard would yell at us. As I said earlier, times then were a lot different.

Come the first of September, Mom enrolled us in school. I was in the first grade and Billy the third. She went with us to register, meet our teachers, and get our supplies, but from that day on she left us on our own to get on with it—again, trusting us to get to school on time each day and do our homework. Although Billy and I did go the first few weeks, we hated giving up our old routine.

We would put our swimsuits on under our school clothes, pick up our books and lunch money, and head for the beach for a quick swim before running to school. Oftentimes we would be tardy. Once in a while, we would be having so much fun in the water that we couldn't stop. We'd say, "Tomorrow we will go to school." But we didn't. We continued to lunch on chocolate bars, popcorn, hamburgers, and soda. Sometimes we'd get comic books. Life was grand!

During the Florida rain showers in the afternoons, we would study our school books. Billy taught me to print my name, to read a little, to count, and to spell a few words. I picked up reading and spelling easily. Soon I could read the comics on my own. As I think back to those carefree days, I do not know how we got away with it for so long. All I remember was the fun and the freedom—and then what came afterward.

Our happy times came to an abrupt halt the evening my mother opened a letter from the school principal. He informed her that we had failed our courses because we had far too many unexcused absences. I can still remember the frozen look on my mother's face as she sat silently, clutching that letter and staring across the room. I was so nervous I could only watch her through the corner of my eye. When my dad came home that night and read the letter, the seriousness of what we had done became even more evident. He stood up and began pacing silently. He was angry. Neither parent said anything to us for what seemed like the longest time.

I feared what was in store for us, remembering the first time I had upset him, when I was really small. He caught me spitting on another little kid in a fight. He jerked me up by my shirt collar, shook me, and smacked me hard. He taught me what it means to fight fair. No, sir, my dad was nobody I wanted to make angry.

He finally sat us down and said we had better learn to control our behavior instead of always thinking about having fun. He told us we'd better develop some willpower and not let our desires keep us from doing our jobs. Our job for the next few years, he explained, was to attend school, to behave ourselves, and to know that any grade below a B was unacceptable. Also, he wanted us to excel in sports. He wanted us to grow up to be successful and good men.

If we did not do as he said, we were sure to grow up to be worthless. He defined worthless as not being able to go to college or hold a good job or have a driver's license, a car, a home, or a family. We would not be able to afford boats and good fishing gear, guns to hunt with, or anything else. We'd end up in debt and maybe in jail.

When he finished talking, we sighed with relief, thinking now that the lecture was over we would be dismissed. But then he took off his belt and proceeded to give us a whipping that burned our rear ends for hours. That whipping, he said, was to help us remember what he had told us. And it did the trick! Whoever it was who said, "Experience is the best teacher," knew what he was talking about.

As I was growing up, I got a few more whippings after that one, but none were ever as memorable. That night in Florida, I had my first epiphany.

4

Back to Kentucky

When we are children we seldom think of the future. This innocence leaves us free to enjoy ourselves as few adults can. The day we fret about the future is the day we leave our childhood behind.

Patrick Rothfuss

Just after Thanksgiving that year, we got word that Grandma was very sick, so we returned to Cynthiana, though my dad hated to leave his job. Billy and I had overheard him and Mom talking about moving again. My mother's brother, Ray Harney, was a saddle horse trainer in a little place called Six Corners, Massachusetts, very near Providence, Rhode Island. He worked for a wealthy businessman, C. P. Casell, and lived in a house on his farm, managing his stables and training his saddle horses to show. My uncle said he thought Dad could find work at a big laundry company in Providence and that we could live with him until we were able to afford a place of our own. So as soon as Grandma recovered, we moved again. Billy and I were happy about traveling to a new place. We didn't realize the worries our parents had.

Mother enrolled us in a little country elementary school a few miles from the farmhouse where we lived. Billy had to repeat the third grade and I the first. We had a great time riding back and forth with the other kids in an old school bus over rutted country roads. And our attendance record was perfect that semester. Everyone was friendly. Some teased us about our Kentucky accents, but it was all in fun. We thought their accents were funny too. Living in

Massachusetts, where the snow fell four or five feet deep that winter, was fantastic. We loved the snow as much as we loved the ocean. We made sleds from scraps of corrugated tin roofing and spent hours sledding. It is a wonder one of us did not get decapitated from the sharp edges on that tin. Our uncle's farmhouse was bordered by woods where there was a den of red foxes. Many times, Billy and I would sit outside quietly for hours watching the red foxes play. My childhood was idyllic.

But before the school year was out, Grandma's health deteriorated again, so we moved back to Cynthiana. This time my parents knew that they could not leave Grandma alone anymore. They would have to find some way to make a living in Cynthiana.

Using the knowledge and experience he had gained from working at dry-cleaning plants in Miami and in Providence, Dad decided to build and operate his own dry-cleaning business. On the empty lot adjacent to our home, he had carpenters construct a framed building that housed machinery to press and store the finished dry clothing. About thirty or so feet away from it, he himself built a smaller building that he covered with corrugated metal at the back of the lot. Outside this little building was a huge, old junk steam engine that he had bought to make steam necessary for his machinery. He made pipes to go from it to the washing machinery in the little building and more pipes to go to the pressing machinery in the larger building. I remember watching him constructing most of that equipment himself in our backyard there on Church Street. Although he did all the plumbing, he hired electricians to do the electrical work. Dad would build a fire in that boiler every day to heat the water to run the presses and the washers, and thus he created and operated Hall's Dry Cleaning.

He also built a small shop at the front of lot and across from our driveway, so Mom had her own business using what she had learned from her job in Miami. Her Ruth Hall's Florist shop was very successful too.

Dad operated his business for many years before he retired

from it and became a postal worker. After a while, he gave that job up for politics and successfully ran for sheriff of Harrison County. He served three terms.

In the late 1930s, my dad bought a used car that had a radio. I remember him sometimes sitting in the car, parked in our driveway, just listening to the radio. After he bought a radio for our home in the early 1940s, Billy and I began listening to all the broadcasts of UK games. That's when our devotion to the Wildcats began. As our interest deepened, we learned to keep score charts on each player. We enjoyed the kids' programs too, especially *Dick Tracy*, *The Shadow*, and *Terry and the Pirates*. I remember Terry was hailed as the "wide awake American Boy."

During the 1937–1938 floods, my dad and a friend, Herman Koffman, went to Cincinnati to help one of their friends. As they were driving through a flooded street, my dad saw a little fox terrier standing alone in the doorway of an empty store. He pulled over as close as he could to the store and yelled to the dog, "Come here, Herman." (Yes, he named him after his friend.) The little dog jumped into the water and swam to the pickup, and Mr. Koffman grabbed him and pulled him in. Dad brought him home for us and the name Herman stuck to him. We all loved him, and he followed Billy and me every time we tried to leave our yard without him. He lived to be eighteen years old.

5

Fishing

There is certainly something in fishing that tends to produce a serenity of mind.

Washington Irving

I have always loved everything and anything that goes on outdoors. And I love every kind of sport. If I had to choose, I'd say fishing is my favorite pastime. From the day I caught my first bass at Griffith's Pond when I was nine, I have loved to fish. Billy and I often went together, with or without our dad, but I went alone many times. The Hall men were good fishermen. We knew the best places to go. One of my favorite places was A. Keller Dam, the site of an old abandoned distillery. Tall weeds had grown around its empty decaying warehouses and barn. A stone house was built right into the stone wall leading to the dam. A game warden lived in it for a while. Later Harry Taylor, a farmer and former UK football player, and his wife lived in it. I remember seeing a big mill wheel lying in the water there. In the twilight, some kids thought the whole site was kind of a creepy place, but it never seemed so to me.

I had seven other good places to fish that I could get to on my bike. They were White Perch Hole, Red Gate, Townsend Creek, Stoner Creek, Indian Creek, South Licking River, and Main Licking. Sometimes I'd catch a nice size mess in regular old farm ponds too.

One time when Billy and I went with our dad, we caught fifty-six crappies, sometimes called new lights. Once we got back home, Dad told us to get busy cleaning them. We dumped them into a big washtub and went to work. After we had scaled and cleaned all but seven, we were so tired we took those seven, still alive, to Betsy Creek near our house and dumped them.

After my sister Laura Jane was born when I was nine years old, I often had to look after her for a few hours during the day while Mom was busy in her florist shop. I was never one who could stay in the house unless I was sick, so I would take Laura Jane with me wherever I went. While she was still a baby, that was not too hard to do. After I got her dressed, I'd plop her down as securely as I could in the basket I had attached to my bike's handle. She was tiny and fit right in, snug as could be. Then off we went. Sounds dangerous, doesn't it? But I was careful and never dropped her.

On one of the afternoons I took her fishing, I caught a whole string of fish in a short time, as many as twenty-five or thirty small fish, and I was worried about how I was going to carry my baby sister, my pole, my bait, and that heavy string of fish while peddling my bike home. I was having enough trouble toting everything up the steep bank to my bike. As I got near the top and could see the highway, a Pepsi-Cola truck driver saw me and waved. He pulled his big truck over onto the grass in a screeching stop and yelled, "Say, boy, would you take 50 cents for all those fish?" Knowing I could buy ten double-dip ice cream cones for 50 cents, and I wouldn't have to clean all those fish, I shouted, "Yes, sir, I sure will!" and whispered, "Thank you, God."

Since then, I have fished in places all over the world and loved every minute of it.

While I was in high school, one of my best fishing buddies was an elderly black man, Jake Lyons, who lived in the last house on the left side of West Pleasant Street, just before you reach the Pleasant Street bridge, if you are going out of Cynthiana. I used to park in front of his house, run onto his porch, where he was often sitting, and ask him to go fishing with me. He'd pick up his gear and off we'd go to A. Keller Dam or some other place. He knew everything about fish, especially crappie. One of the most useful things he taught me was to fish at places that had trees or a tree growing really close to the edge of the water or trees or branches that had been blown into the water. He taught me to shake a branch that hung over the water or shake a fallen trunk of tree or a limb lying in the water. When the leaves, berries, and twigs, and maybe insects would drop into the water, fish would rush to see what was causing all the activity, thinking food—flies, bugs, and such—had fallen in. And fish are always looking for food, of course. Then all I had to do was drop my line in that area and catch a good mess of crappies. The important thing, my buddy emphasized, is to make the fish curious enough to come see what's going on.

Years ago, in the spring, after the NCAA finals were over, Katharine and I enjoyed spending a few days at a fishing camp in Ontario, Canada. Other couples we knew from Lexington and central Kentucky would go there at the same time, and we would all get together. It was a great place to relax, enjoy beautiful scenery, fish, and visit with friends.

Every morning, each couple was assigned a native Indian guide and a boat. The guides would have a predetermined time and place for us to meet for lunch, which they called "shore lunch." It consisted of the fish that had been caught that morning along with some fresh vegetables, and was served to us outdoors on the shore. Those meals tasted so good, as nearly all foods do when eaten outside in a beautiful location. I have such great memories of our visits there.

On one of our earliest trips to that camp, I had an opportunity to teach my guide what old Jake Lyons had taught me as a teenager about catching crappie. One morning, as Louie, our guide, was getting ready to take us down-lake to fish, I said to him, "Louie, do you have any crappie around here?" When he nodded yes, I told him, "Good! Let's see if we can find a fallen tree or a branch lying in the water." He soon spotted one and stopped the boat about twenty or thirty feet from it. We started throwing our baits close to the tree, but we could not throw into it because we'd get our lines hung. Well, we didn't catch anything, didn't even get a nibble. After a while, I said, "Okay, Louie, let's go right up to the tree." He looked at me and shook his head. "No, no, scare fish." I said, "No, we won't. Take us over there and tie us up to the trunk so I can shake that big branch." He made it clear he thought it was a foolish idea and mumbled again, "Scare fish." After he did what I asked him, I stood up in the boat and with my foot I shook a branch and then dropped my line in. In hardly any time at all, we had caught more than a dozen of the finest black crappies we had ever seen. And for our shore lunch that day, we all dined on delicious black crappies.

Okay, I am bragging here, but I am proud to say that I did teach an expert Indian guide how to fish for crappie by using old Jake Lyons's advice.

6

Teenage Years

When my brother Billy got to be a teenager, our relationship changed dramatically. Until then, we had done nearly everything together for so long that I couldn't understand why he no longer wanted to. He was my best friend. But when he began acquiring new friends his own age, they did not want a little brother trailing along after them. Whenever I saw him preparing to leave the house, I got ready to follow him into town. It made me sad and mad when Billy refused to let me go with him. Many a day we'd fight and yell at each other all the way down the street because I had insisted on following him. I think perhaps my closeness to my brother when I was small led me to make friends with many older students once I was at UK.

After I got to junior high school and made new friends, I did not miss being with Billy so much anymore. I made even more friends after I started playing in organized sports and had some success. I was developing my own identity and enjoying doing so.

Before I could sign up for junior varsity basketball, I had to have my first physical examination. The doctor told my mother that I was healthy enough, but very thin. My mother explained to him that I had a great appetite and ate well. The only reason I was thin, she said, was that I was in perpetual motion. "He won't sit down even to eat his meals for thinking about all the things he wants to do."

After the doctor examined my eyes, he surprised us when he said I had poor eyesight. I was not aware that I was not seeing well and said so. The doctor explained that whenever we are born with a deficiency of some kind, our bodies help us to adjust to it, and we may grow up not even being aware of what is missing. That's why I thought I had been seeing the same as everyone else—that is, until I put on my first pair of prescription glasses.

What a tremendous difference glasses made. I remember looking around and seeing details of things that I had not known existed—like the individual leaves on trees and the different colors of leaves. I had never seen individual leaves before. Trees had always looked like thick bushes to me. With glasses, I could read with ease, and reading became a lifelong pleasure. I had always made merely average grades before, but with glasses my studies were so much easier. I made the honor roll every semester after my vision improved.

No matter what I was doing, I committed myself to the task and wanted to be best at it. My dad may have instilled that idea in me, I suppose. He urged me to set goals for myself and work toward achieving them. He told me not to quit until I had accomplished my goal. He preached that nothing happens without effort, so I worked hard at everything I undertook. I was in the Beta Club and in the Boy Scouts. Our Scout meetings were held every Monday night at the city hall, where there was a basketball court. After the meetings, we would play basketball for as long as we were allowed, and then we ran to my friend Billy Fitzgerald's house and played there. Billy had a goal in his yard, which was close enough to the hospital parking lot that we could see to play basketball at night by the hospital lights. I did not have a goal at my house, but I did have my own basketball.

My first organized athletic experience was playing basketball in the seventh and eighth grades. Wearing glasses became a small problem then. I used to tape them to my temples, but I still ended up breaking several pairs. Contact lenses were not available then. When playing football, I wore goggles.

Our junior varsity basketball coach was Larkie Box, a Marine veteran of World War II. He was a great friend, and didn't seem to mind my tagging along after him. He mentored me in sports and also in life in general. He even taught me to drive. He had graduated from Cynthiana High School, where he had been a star basketball and football player. After he emphasized the importance of strengthening exercises, I started lifting weights and running. I made my own weights by filling two large cans connected by a bar with concrete. After the concrete set, I had my own barbell. For chin-ups, I put a pipe in a tree in my backyard. I worked out every day too.

I will never forget the time I was leaving the Youth Center downtown when Larkie came riding up, without a saddle, on an old horse. He told me to hop on, he'd take me home. Parts of Cynthiana are hilly; as we were headed up the hill to my house, the old horse slipped and Larkie and I slid to the ground. The horse ran off while Larkie and I sat on the curb laughing—along with a number of spectators.

The summer before I started my freshman year in high school, I lived with my uncle and helped him with his farm work. I no longer had to lift weights. I got plenty of weight-lifting exercise in the hayfield and the tobacco patch. I was stronger than I'd ever been and ready for football practice, which started two weeks before school began. After finishing my work on the farm, I went to football practice at night, playing under the lights. Because of all the lifting, hoeing, shoveling, and pulling work I did on the farm, I was in better shape than many of my teammates. Our football coach Bill Boswell told me that.

School was one mile away from my house and for lunch I would run home and back. School let out at five minutes to 12:00 and the town noon siren went off at exactly 12:00. The moment the school bell rang, I would leap from my desk and dash home, running the quickest, most direct route, which meant jumping hedges and cutting across yards. Every time I would get home before the siren sounded.

By the time I was a senior, I had saved enough money to buy a 1915 Model T Ford that I drove to school every day. Using our school colors, I painted the body green with big white dots. Three of my buddies who lived in my neighborhood rode with me. The school was on a hill. I parked across the street from it, facing downhill with a chock (a fireplace-size log) behind the back wheel to keep my car from rolling down the street. We worked out an efficient system for when we were going home for lunch: one kid grabbed the water can (I always carried one because the radiator leaked) and filled the radiator; another boy grabbed the crank and cranked the motor; I jumped into the driver's seat and started the engine. The last boy grabbed the chock away from the back wheel and off we went, sputtering and rattling down the street!

I had so many boys riding with me to football practice that I had a hard time getting up the hill to the football field. So I drove up backward because my old car was stronger in reverse. Sometimes the boys had to get out and push that old car up the hill.

7

Football

Football is a great deal like life in that it teaches that work, sacrifice, perseverance, competitive drive, selflessness and respect for authority is the price that each and every one of us must pay to achieve any goal that is worthwhile.

Vince Lombardi

I love football. In high school, I loved going to practice and to games. I love watching it being played. I like the challenge, the hitting, the physical part of it. Our head coach was Bill Boswell, a mild-mannered gentleman, who seemed to care about each of us as individuals. He was demanding but always fair. I was the only freshman on the varsity team, and he groomed me to be the quarterback. He gave me a book to study on what a quarterback should and should not do. One of my greatest honors is to be included in the Cynthiana High School Football Hall of Fame.

Football in the 1940s was not as scientific as it today. I did the kickoff, the punting, called the offensive play as a quarterback, and I called the defensive signals from my linebacker position. I also received punts and kickoffs, so I had lots to work on in practice. I played in my first high school game when I was in the eighth grade. At that time, I was about five feet, two inches tall and weighed eighty-six pounds. I participated in only a couple of plays because the other players did not throw me the ball. My freshman year I was a substitute quarterback. My sophomore, junior, and senior year I was a starting quarterback. As a sophomore I also played safety on defense; my junior year I played halfback on defense.

In my senior year Coach Boswell retired and was replaced by Red Rocke. At the start of spring practice, a regular linebacker had the mumps and missed practice, so I saw an opportunity and took it. I had always wanted to play linebacker, so I simply told Coach Rocke that I *was* linebacker. He let me play in that role the rest of the time.

All of us on the team were competitive. During my senior year our record was six wins, one loss, and one tie. The second game of that senior year, against Paris, I got a late hit after I released a pass, and my left knee buckled. I stayed in the game and threw a touchdown pass to give us an 18-12 victory over Paris.

The next Monday I came to practice and tried to run a quarterback spinner when my leg just gave way under me. The coach checked my knee and sent me to Dr. Todd Smiser, who took one look and said, "You've got water on the knee, probably torn ligaments and cartilage damage. Lay off practice for a while." I did not practice the whole week. But Friday night I dressed out for the game against Carlisle. While I sat on the bench, a substitute quarterback started the game. I was not expecting to play that night. On the first possession, he fumbled and Coach walked down the bench and asked if I thought I could play. Dr. Smiser had already taped my knee pre-game, so Coach Rocke told me not to run the ball but said I could pass and kick, just not receive kickoffs or punts. I went into the game and played, and then played every down the rest of the year offensively and defensively with a fitted leather brace supported by steel and hinges. I could still kick and throw and play my linebacker position. I never carried the ball until the last game, but I passed, punted, and kicked off. I played my defensive linebacker position. In the last game against Georgetown, I ran for two touchdowns. One was called back for penalty, but for the second one, I ran for fifteen yards.

I loved football and wanted to play in college, but when Coach Rupp gave me a chance to play basketball for UK, I could not turn him down.

8

My Early Influences
and Role Models

Setting an example is not the main means of influencing
others; it is the only means.

Albert Einstein

In my freshman year at Cynthiana High, I was a substitute on the
varsity basketball team and then a starter in my sophomore year.
My coach was Kelly "Pop" Stanfield, who was one of the winningest
coaches ever, but he never got the recognition he deserved because
he never made it to the finals. The regionals were as far as he ever
went, but he went every year. I don't think he lost more than five
games in any one season. But in the finals, Maysville or Brookville
always beat us. Coach Stanfield was a gentleman and one of my
mentors. He showed us how to be good citizens and taught us about
sportsmanship.

Although I loved playing football, my career has been in
basketball, which seemed more suited to my skills and my size. Also,
it requires only a ball and a basket of some kind, and any kid with
those two items can play alone any time he wants. It is more fun
to have someone else to play with, but it is not necessary. I used to
practice shooting for long periods at a time alone.

In the summers someone would organize games, and I played
in them whenever and wherever I could. I played so much that I
got pretty good at the game by the time I entered high school. At
school I lettered three years in football and in basketball. I captained
both teams my senior year, and I still stayed on the honor roll every
semester. Although I never campaigned for the job or even wanted

it, my classmates elected me class president for all four years. I guess they couldn't get anybody else to take the office. My high school years were some of the happiest in my life.

My junior year I had a huge surprise. I met Coach Rupp and Coach Harry Lancaster briefly for the first time. They had come to Cynthiana High to observe two of our seniors and high scorers, Paul Hicks and Cavin Barnett. That night I scored seven points in the first half and then broke my glasses, which I had taped to my temples. Then in the second half I scored thirteen points playing without my glasses. Go figure.

After the game I was in the locker room when a classmate rushed in saying that the UK coaches wanted to meet me too before they left. I couldn't believe it. Me? I looked out in the gym and saw Coach Rupp surrounded by a crowd. I took a deep breath, straightened my shoulders, spit in the palm of my hand, and smoothed my hair down. Then I walked over to him, and with a tremble in my voice, I uttered, "Excuse me, sir, Coach Rupp, I am Joe B. Hall." He reached out and shook my hand vigorously and smiled, repeating my name. Coach Rupp was impressive in every way—the way he looked, the way he stood up straight with his legs apart, the way he spoke. He was tall and looked strong. He was dressed in a dark suit, white shirt, and tie. I don't remember the color of his suit, but it wasn't brown. I had already been told he wore his brown suit and red socks only to games. While he was talking to me, he looked straight at me and spoke in a voice that surprised me. There was an old southern, high-pitched nasal tone to his voice. He emphasized some words by dragging them out, and sometimes after he said something he looked at me intently to see if I were taking it all in. He was like no one else I have ever met.

After he introduced me to Coach Lancaster, he told me how grand it is to play for the best team in the best program with the best coaches the world has ever known—the University of Kentucky Wildcats. He urged me to think about doing just that. Think about it?! Man, that's all I did after that! Although I was with him for no more than a couple of minutes, I knew I had been in the presence of greatness. And this important person had wanted to see me—me! Little did I know then the huge role he would play in my life later on.

I had so many advantages growing up when and where I did. During the Depression and then World War II, we learned to save and to make do or do without. I watched my dad and uncles repair broken equipment and tools that were too expensive to replace. During those hard times, we all learned to work together.

In a small town like Cynthiana, where nearly everyone knew everyone else, people looked after one another. All the businesses— the farm implement, hardware, grocery, and drug stores as well as shops of all kinds, cafes, and restaurants—were owned and run by local people who cared about their customers. The carpenters, builders, plumbers, and so on were our neighbors, relatives, and friends. They all wanted to provide the best services they could, and they did. Although there surely must have been some crime in Cynthiana, as there is everywhere, it was very rare.

I was thirteen years old when World War II started, and I remember how patriotism permeated every aspect of our lives then. Movies, books, art, music, sports, radio programs, churches, businesses, schools, and even cartoons were all somehow war-related. Patriotic posters were in all the storefronts and on the walls of all public and some private buildings. I remember one slogan well: "If you do with less, our soldiers will have more!"

I remember the ration/stamp books the government issued once a month to every person or family, allowing each a certain amount of food, gasoline, and other things. Products were purchased with cash and with these stamps. Once you had used all your stamp book allotment for, say, flour, then you had to wait until the next month to get more stamps for flour. Whenever my mom went shopping, she carried her ration books with her. I remember that sugar was especially expensive and scarce, and how Grandma experimented with different kinds of sweeteners, like syrup, to make pies and cakes. Just about everyone had a vegetable garden. They were called Victory Gardens. We did not have one because my uncle, who had a farm, raised enough vegetables for us too. I can remember my grandma and my mom steaming up our kitchen in the summer canning as many fruits and vegetables as they could.

Gasoline and oil were rationed. Since it was nearly impossible to get new tires, the technique of vulcanizing tires and tubes became necessary. Vulcanizing was a procedure that used heat to press a patch over holes in tubes and tires to reseal them. It required special equipment and some training. It made the tires and tubes reusable, keeping many cars and trucks running.

Growing up watching my family and others being thrifty, repairing things that broke down rather than rushing out to buy new ones, taught me lessons I would never have known had I been reared in more privileged circumstances. I was blessed to have the kind of upbringing I did. My parents let me learn the hard way that some things are just a lot better to do or not to do than other things. As I mentioned earlier, they took care of our needs, but they let us work and save to buy our wants. Their cardinal rules were "Don't get into fights, mind your manners, and be home by suppertime."

I was blessed also with good male role models—my father, my uncles, my brother Bill, my high school coaches Kelly Stanfield, Larkie Box, Bill Boswell, Red Rocke, and Judge Mac Swinford, father of my good friend John Swinford. Those men trained me to work hard and to be competitive and disciplined. Although they corrected me plenty of times and showed me better ways to do whatever I was trying to do, they never belittled me. Winners, they taught, were those who had prepared themselves better than their opponents had. That idea stayed with me. I understood that if I wanted to be a successful lawyer or preacher or whatever, I had better make the commitment to being the best. I had to prepare to do the job.

They also taught me that failure can be a good thing if one

learns from it. I never thought I was so good that I could succeed or excel at anything I tried to do without hard work. I knew that if I failed, it likely meant that the other guy had been better prepared than I. But if I had earnestly done the best I could and still lost, then I was simply not as good as my opponent. There is no shame in losing like that, but if I had not been thoroughly prepared, well, shame on me.

The word *honorable* is old-fashioned. It is not a word we hear used much anymore in describing someone's character, and that's a pity. The men who influenced me as I was growing up were all honorable men, and I am grateful they were part of my life.

9

About Working

Without ambition, one starts nothing. Without work, one finishes nothing. The prize will not be sent to you. You have to win it.

Ralph Waldo Emerson

I like to work, and I like to work hard, and then see my accomplishments. While I was growing up, I had all kinds of jobs. When I was really small, I stood on a stool and washed dishes at the Dixie Ice Cream Bar for 22 cents an hour. Then I was an usher in the theater, where I swept the floors and picked up the trash. When I was fifteen years old, I said I was sixteen so that the Rural Electric Association would hire me to dig holes and trim right-of-ways. We didn't have power saws in those days. We used a two-man crosscut saw and axes.

When I was a senior in high school, I was put in charge of the Cynthiana swimming pool. Before the pool opened, the Red Cross sent me to Lake Oliver, Indiana, to take water safety classes. I learned to teach people how to swim and to be lifeguards. When I returned, I taught the potential lifeguards in an old quarry on the edge of town. I don't think we tested the water, but luckily none of us came down with typhoid fever. I do remember telling the boys to swim fast past the rock piles because often there were big snakes there.

During the summers, I liked helping my uncle on his farm doing whatever he needed done. I learned so much from him. One time I recruited some of my high school football player friends to help him and me strip bluegrass seeds. I worked for other people too. One year a farmer had me put in his tobacco crop. I hired some guys to work with me. We were being paid by the hour, and one of the boys told me we shouldn't be in such a hurry to finish, that we ought to slow down so we'd make more money. I told him no, that we would continue as we had been and that he could leave if he wanted. Later that same guy asked me to put his crop in while he was on his honeymoon. I asked him, "Are you okay with my doing as you suggested we do on that other job we had?"

The summer before I was to enroll at the University of Kentucky, I learned that the farmers in my county were looking for help bailing their hay. I saw that as an opportunity to make some money. Without telling my parents or anyone else, I borrowed enough from the bank to buy an old truck. Then I went to Lemons Farm Equipment to buy a bailer. Mr. Lemons took me out in the yard and showed me a pickup bailer for $1,200. I asked if he had something less expensive. He then showed me one that had welding scars and needed work. He wanted $600 for it. "Mr. Lemons," I asked, "don't you have something for much, much less?" He said, "As a matter of fact, I do." I followed him to the back of the lot near the fence and he showed me an old Case tuck bailer. He told me, "Joe, you can have this if you haul it off my lot."

That afternoon I bought a used Wisconsin engine and mounted it to the bailer. *Bingo!* It worked! I was ready to bail straw out of straw stacks. The horse farmers liked tucked-bailed straw better because it was springier and had no cut wire pieces in it to choke their horses.

My good friend John Swinford and three other guys I played football with wanted to work with me, and a couple of farmers joined us. I organized them into a team of pushers, feeders, and wire tie-ers and told them, "We will work from 'can't see' to 'can't see' for $3 a day, and bring your own lunch." We went from farm to farm throughout the county bailing straw for farmers who needed us. We bailed mainly straw out of straw stacks behind a thrashing machine. We put in a full day every day in the hottest July ever until we had done all the farms. We worked so efficiently and hard that some farmers and their families came out to watch us. When we finished all our bailing, I had earned more money than I ever had before. After I paid my workers, my few expenses, and my debt to the bank, I had plenty left over to help me with my college expenses that year.

10

Wildcats' World, 1944–1947

> The invention of basketball was not an accident. It was
> developed to meet a need. Those boys simply would not play
> "Drop the Handkerchief."
>
> James Naismith

As kids, my brother and I were in awe of the Wildcats. We followed every Kentucky team as far back as I can remember, way back to when I was only ten or eleven years old. We never got to go to any of the UK games, though, until I attended the university. Tickets to the games were hard to get even then and expensive. Coach Rupp had made basketball extremely popular in Kentucky.

In the early 1940s, I followed players such as Ermal Allen, Bob Brannum, and Milt Ticco. Billy and I would sit cross-legged on our bed listening to the broadcast games on a little radio that Dad had bought for us to keep in our room. We would try to play right along with the teams by tossing paper wads into empty coffee cans we had propped up on the bed. We started keeping track of the points scored in every game and recorded how many points each player had. We tried to record rebounds too, but the broadcasting in those days was not always good—lots of static.

I remember the first time I went to the Kentucky Boys State Tournament. It was in 1944 and it was played in the Alumni Gym. I was fifteen years old. The gym was packed. After Coach Rupp introduced Kentucky to his fast-break style of playing in the 1930s, the game became so popular that the university had to station football players as security guards at the entrances to the old gym.

31

Throngs of Lexington people who hadn't bought season tickets but wanted to attend home games would show up. They got very angry when they were told tickets were sold out. They did not take that news too nicely, and police had to stay around to keep order. The doors had to be kept open for ventilation because there was no air-conditioning in those days and so many people smoked cigarettes then. I don't know how we stood all that smoke.

During that state tournament game, the doors at both ends of the Alumni Gym were left open and guarded by some UK players. My heroes—Wilbur Shu, Jack Tingle, Jack Parkinson, and some others whose names I had learned from listening to the radio—were door guards that night. They were all tall guys. Billy and I, along with a couple of other kids, stood silently right next to them, staring up at them adoringly. We were too scared to talk to any of them. Just breathing the same air was thrilling enough.

I remember that tournament well. The Harlan team, coached by Joe Gilley, beat Dayton 40–28. All-American Wallace Jones was the team's lead player. His nickname was Wah Wah because his baby sister could not say Wallace. He turned out to be an all-time, all-round great athlete excelling in football, baseball, basketball, and track at UK. Another guard on the Harlan team was Humsey Yessin, who was later a manager for the UK basketball team. The Harlan uniforms were the same colors as ours at Cynthiana High— green and white. I had no idea then that in just three years I would be a member of the Wildcats and friends with Wah Wah. He was a great guy.

That tournament was as close as I ever got to any UK player until the summer of 1947. I could only imagine how wonderful it would be to be a member of the team.

After my high school graduation, I couldn't decide what I wanted to major in when I got to college. I was considering law or the ministry. Then that summer, I was blessed with an invitation to try out for the Wildcats before the fall semester started.

The practices were held in the old Alumni Gym, which at

that time was the varsity gym. Prospective players had come in by bus, train, or car with their parents from all over Kentucky and the surrounding states. These tryouts were legal back then, but they are not today. Now kids are judged by how well they play in their high school games.

The day would start with UK student and team manager Humsey Yessin reading the names of the boys who would play on opposing teams. Those teams would scrimmage for fifteen or twenty minutes while assistant coach Harry Lancaster, Humsey, and sometimes Coach Rupp too would watch. Then ten more names would be called and so on until we all had played. At the end of the day, Humsey read the names of ten players invited to return the next week. My name was called. I played only two weeks of those tryouts and was one of the final four selected to go to the University of Kentucky. I had been chosen to play on the East All Star Team in the East/West All Star game coached by Earle Jones of Maysville. In the practice the day before the game, I sprained my ankle and was able to make only a token appearance. But I had done well in the practice sessions, and my performance won me a scholarship to the university and made me a member of the Wildcats' team. Sprained ankle or no, I was walking on air.

11

A UK Freshman

The direction in which education starts a man will determine
his future life.

Plato

My spirits were high that fall of 1947 when I enrolled in the
University of Kentucky with a pre-law major. I was excited
about being on the Wildcats team even though I could not play ball
that year because NCAA regulations did not allow Division One
schools to let students play their first year unless they had enrolled
in the summer. The other three freshmen could play because they
had enrolled in the summer. I was the only nonplaying freshman
that year, but I was expected to go to practice every day. I was okay
with that because I believed I would be a much stronger and better
player as a sophomore.

Everything went along great that freshman year. The football
players lived in houses while we lived in the dorms. I roomed with
Jim Line and Roger Day in the old Kincaid Hall. We lived in a suite
that had a study room and a bedroom. We used the community
bathroom down the hall to shower. We had our meals in the
Student Union cafeteria with the football players. Jim, Roger, and
I all got along well and became good friends. Jim Line was one of
the finest men I ever knew and surely the most studious. He was
majoring in physics and stayed up late every night studying. He
did not have any reason to help a freshman like me, but he did. Jim
showed me around campus and downtown Lexington. He told me
what to expect from certain professors and the coaches. I thought
a lot of Roger Day too. Other friends were Ken Campbell, who

roomed with Ralph Beard and Humsey Yessin on the floor below ours. Ken often came home with me on weekends to work with me on my uncle's farm and to eat my mom's good cooking.

Our practices were held in the Alumni Gym where we shared a small training room with the football team. We had our own dressing room downstairs in the gym across from the football players'. We all got to be pals and rooted for each other. After we finished our practice, we would go out on the field across the street and watch football practice. Coach Bear Bryant was really tough on those boys. He was much like Coach Rupp in many ways, but he was physically a much stronger man. Whenever he demonstrated an aggressive technique of hitting, he'd hurt that kid. Although we were dead tired after our practices, the football players were totally exhausted after theirs. After they limped back to the gym, they would lie down in the showers and let the warm water soothe their sore bodies.

Long before practice sessions started officially in mid-October, we had heard many stories about Coach Rupp. We were told about his silence requirement. The older players warned us beginners to be silent going into the gym, that Coach Rupp's motto was "Unless you can improve on silence, do not speak." To show you how serious he was about maintaining silence: one time his celebrity friend Albert B. Chandler, nicknamed Happy, was visiting practice and started talking to someone in the gym. He had been lieutenant governor, governor, US senator, and he was commissioner of major league baseball at the time Coach Rupp screamed at him to shut up or get out of the gym.

Silence was required because he wanted us to focus entirely on what we had to do and on what he had to say. We were not to talk, whisper, whistle, hum, giggle, laugh, clap, clown around, or touch each other—and above all else we had to be on time. "He'll lock the doors if you're late," the older players warned, adding, "Oh, yeah, don't ever dribble the ball while he's talking!"

They also told us to be prepared for some sarcastic criticism laced with profanity after we made mistakes. Yes, Coach Rupp was by then famous for his creative and masterful use of the language. He had some unique but hurtful ways of correcting us. Remember this, though, the older players added: when he or Harry cussed us out that meant they thought we were or would be capable of playing for the Wildcats. "It's when they ignore you that you need to worry about getting kicked off the team. Most of the time you're going to feel sorry for the guy he's criticizing, but don't say anything to him or pat him on the back."

Sometimes you wanted to laugh at some of the things Coach Rupp said or the expressions on his face. One time when he got upset at us in practice he yelled: "Burn this place down. Don't burn the libraries! Or the student center! Or the science building! Just burn this damn place down to the ground! We don't need it if turds like you are all we can get." It was so hard not to laugh when he did things like this. Coach Rupp could be hilarious unintentionally. But we didn't dare laugh—unless he was laughing.

12

First Practice, 1947

The goal is to make practice more difficult physically and
mentally than anything your players will face during a game.
Bob Knight

When I entered the gym for my first practice and saw Coach
Adolph Rupp, I thought my heart was going to pound right
out of my chest. He was forty-five years old then, tall, stocky, and
tan. He had a very wide forehead and a receding hairline. His dark
hair was parted on the side and just beginning to gray. He was
standing erect near the wall under one basket with his arms folded
across his chest and legs spread apart. His lips were thin, tightly
closed, and they slanted down in the corners, giving him a serious
expression. His eyes were dark brown and piercing.

At the other end of the floor under the basket, his first assistant
coach Harry Lancaster stood in the same position. He was about
ten years younger than Coach Rupp and was built just about the
same way and was about the same size, only a little shorter and
much stronger looking. He had dark hair that he wore in a crew
cut or what they called a "flat top" then. The two were silently
waiting for us. We had been told that Coach Rupp and Harry had
known each other for a long time and worked together well, but
Coach Rupp was always in charge. For practices, we dressed in
white shorts, socks, and white undershirts. The coaches dressed in
starched military khaki outfits, and they looked and acted like drill
sergeants. They demanded attention and discipline.

Coach Rupp started out by telling us that once we put on our
Kentucky blue and white uniforms we were special. We represented

the great University of Kentucky, and we had better represent her as "cham-*pee*-ions!" He had a certain way of drawing out some syllables when he wanted to emphasize a point. He went on to stress that we *would* know the fundamentals of basketball so well, and we *would* have so much intelligence, stamina, strength, and ability that we *would* play basketball better than anyone else.

We learned that first day that winning was everything for Coach Rupp, and he wanted us to have the same strong desire to win he had. Winning, he said, builds character. You win by playing better than anyone else. "Your *sole* purpose in life here at the University of Kentucky is to score points in every game, to be better than anyone else on that floor," he told us. "You forget that crap about sportsmanship! If basketball is all about sportsmanship, then why in the hell is that scoreboard up there? Why do they keep score, huh?"

As we soon learned, he often used variations of biblical statements, such as "He who controlleth the backboard, controlleth the game. Remember that!" He stated his philosophy succinctly when he said, "I know that I have plenty of enemies, but I'd rather be the most-hated winning coach in the country than the most popular losing one." And he was!

One of the maintenance workers, an older guy, told us that Coach Rupp got the idea for wearing those khaki uniforms when he and Harry were in France in 1945. Harry served as the recreation officer while he was in the navy. He coached softball and baseball. During that same time, the armed forces had invited Rupp to France to conduct some basketball clinics for the USO. It was then that Rupp got the idea of conducting basketball practices in military attire, and he bought enough khaki outfits at the PX to last him a long time. After they returned to the States in 1946, Coach Rupp hired Lancaster as his first assistant coach. They worked well together and seemed to have the same type of personality.

Practice started at 2:00 sharp and ended at 3:30, occasionally later. Sometimes the assistant coach would take over after the main practice and work us longer. Every day Coach Rupp presented us with a schedule of drills we were to do that day. He had a drawer full of these drills and kept making new ones. He started every practice having us first shoot free throws for a few minutes, and then individual position shots for about thirty minutes. We had to do them perfectly. He emphasized repetition. He believed that if a player performed the same maneuver over and over and over correctly, it would become an automatic act for him to do it perfectly in every game. He operated practices by a time clock. He was highly organized. He emphasized offense. He liked a tight man-to-man defense, not zone, because he could single a player out for criticism if the man that he was guarding scored points. He would put all of our names up on the board after a game and painfully humiliate any one of us whose man had scored points. He was merciless in his criticism.

In 1947–1948 he had us start working hard on defense about two weeks before our first game. Later he would change his routine and do it earlier. Defense, he said, is like spreading manure: "It's a dirty job but somebody has to do it." These practices were grueling, too.

During a short break early on he stopped us to talk about his "rules." We had already been given a typed copy of them at our first squad meeting, when they had been discussed. Nevertheless, for emphasis, I suppose, he reminded us that we had to keep a 2.0 grade point average; we had to be on time to every class; we were not to cut classes; we had to be in our dorm rooms by 11:00 p.m., and lights had to be out at midnight on weekdays; we had to avoid playing cards and using alcohol or tobacco; we had to keep ourselves clean and properly groomed; we had to get his permission if we wanted to leave the city limits. Further, he stressed that we should never, ever talk to sportswriters or radio people or do interviews without his prior knowledge and permission.

Of course, he would talk to us about upcoming games and travel plans. Occasionally he would rant on about girls and dating.

He hated for us to have romances. Girls, he said, were major distractions, and he strongly discouraged us from associating with them. He never, never, ever wanted to see any co-eds hanging around the gym waiting for us, or hanging on us.

However, he never checked that we were following his rules. To my knowledge, he never visited our dorms at night to see if we were in by 11:00. The only thing he scrutinized every single day was our cafeteria charges. He watched our account sheets like a hawk. He was as tight as the bark on a tree, and that was his budget he was protecting.

Whenever we were in his presence, we had to stay sharp and focused on what we were doing. We always had this dreadful fear of being replaced. There were always plenty of guys wanting and waiting to take our place. If one of us made a mistake, he'd jump on him as if he were a recruit with his tie on backward. Then we had to listen to him spew his caustic insults. I remember one time when we were having an especially bad day, although we'd been working really hard, Coach Rupp yelled, "Cease! Cease! Oh, my Gawd, I have never seen such a poor performance. This is the worst practice I have ever seen." He walked to the center of the floor, knelt on one knee, and wiped something off the floor with his finger. He raised his hand and looked at it, saying loudly, "Well, lookee there—it's a drop of sweat. I guess one of the janitors sweeping the floor must have dropped it."

Nobody wanted to be the object of his wrath. Whenever he jumped on one of us, we all felt it. One day I felt especially sorry for my roommate Jim Line, who was softly whistling a tune to himself as he approached the gym. He was doing it unconsciously, but Coach Rupp in the gym could hear the faint whistling and shouted, "Harry, who's doing that whistling? Who is it? We play basketball here, not music! Tell that little —— to get out right now and go to the music department." No one tattled on Jim, so he went on to practice.

Another time he told a kid, "I want you to act nonchalant, like you don't know what's going on, and then break behind the screen to get the ball. Ah, hell, just act natural and it's bound to work." He would briefly thank us when we won for adding another victory to our record and then go into a lengthy discussion about our mistakes.

By the time I was there, Coach Rupp was already famous for his clever use of language, for his phrasing of sarcastic remarks that he could create on the spur of the moment. And, oh, yes, some of them were directed at me, too. Contact lenses were still not available. Another boy and I were the only ones who wore glasses. I taped mine to my temples. One day my glasses broke. Coach Rupp yelled a string of expletives at me and said, "Now we know what we do with Hall. Let's put a rope around him and let Hill [another player] drag him around."

Another time, when I messed up on a drill, Coach Rupp was furious. He yelled, "Hall, you just made the *worst* mistake that's ever been made in this gym! The *worst*, do you hear me? Oh, my Gawd, if you did that in a game I would take you to the dressing room and shoot you dead. No! By damn, I would shoot you right here in front of everybody." I had heartburn for days after that.

If anyone missed a practice, that was terrible because the next day he might be at the bottom of the list of team members or even scratched off the team. An injury or illness could cost a player his position on the team. It was all so competitive. We had to stay healthy and be fully present, mentally and physically.

When I had to have a tonsillectomy, I chose to have the surgery on a Friday, thinking I'd be back at practice on Monday. Well, I didn't get back until Wednesday, and even that was too soon. A hemorrhage put me back in the hospital. The whole time I was recuperating, I worried that I'd never get caught up. Another time I sprained my ankle. After I returned from both sick leaves, I got permission to stay late after each practice and continue working. There was no way ever that Coach Rupp could not have known that I was sincere and doing all that I could to stay in his program. He knew.

I have often wondered why Coach Rupp did and said some of the terrible things he did. I respected him for his remarkable achievements, though. He had succeeded in doing what every coach dreams of doing: winning. I learned so much from him. I kept notes almost daily of our practices and made diagrams of his various drills and instructions. Those notes were useful later after I started coaching. I used some of his techniques but developed many more of my own. I never tried to imitate him, never wanted to. He was one of a kind, for sure. I never knew anyone like him before or since.

A contrast to Coach Rupp would be Hank Iba, a prince of a man. Mr. Iba had a sweet, kind way about him that impressed everyone who knew him. Whenever he walked into a hotel, restaurant, or stadium, he was just as polite to the janitors, housekeepers, waiters, bellhops, and so on as he was to the administrators and the hierarchy. He was not just a great coach, he was a great person. When I think of him, I think of that line "The greater the man, the greater the courtesy." I believe the poet Tennyson said that.

My personality is totally different from Coach Rupp's, as many newspaper sportswriters have been quick to point out. He was quotable; I was not. He was fodder for the media; I was not. He has been described as brilliant, egotistical, entertaining, clever, insulting, and vain, whereas I have been described as reserved, polite, and mild-mannered. One reporter wrote that I was "boring." Why, when I as a young coach walked into a gym, many people thought my manager was the coach.

When I started out at UK in 1947, I was eighteen and naive. I was not used to the likes of Coaches Rupp and Lancaster. Neither behaved or spoke like any of my previous coaches, who corrected us but never demeaned or insulted us. They were not even like any of the men I had known thus far. Neither Coach Rupp nor Harry ever engaged in any friendly chit-chat with us before or after practice, and they rarely gave any of us a pat on the back, smile, or thumbs up. In their ordinary speech, they incorporated all the cuss words they could pack into their sentences.

Now don't get the impression that I was a prude or was so delicate then that I was shocked by their crude language. No, indeed, I had grown up working on farms where I heard plenty of barnyard smutty language from some farmers and farmhands. I just did not expect to hear it so glibly flying off the tongues of the University of Kentucky coaches. I did then and I still do occasionally cuss, but there are some words I have never used and never will. My favorite swear word has always been *horseshit*, but in some circles, horseshit is not necessarily an expletive—not when we think of all the fine Thoroughbred horses we have here in Lexington.

It did not take me long to learn that Coach Rupp was only tough talking, not tough physically. Even his hands were soft. He wouldn't fight anyone; he couldn't fight. It frightened him whenever anyone threatened to attack him, and he always wanted Harry near him. Harry was an ex-military man, strong and not afraid of anybody. He would fight at the drop of a hat. Coach Rupp relied on Harry to protect him, and he had to do so on more than one occasion, too.

One of Harry's favorite "Adolph stories" was about the time they were playing a game in Chicago, and he found Adolph in the locker room being smashed against the wall by an angry stranger. Harry pulled the guy off and pitched him out into the hall. The guy sprang back and again tried to hit Coach Rupp, so Harry grabbed him and knocked him out cold, breaking his own finger in doing so. Later on he was amused to learn that Coach Rupp was boasting about how he had clobbered his attacker. As he told his version of the incident, Coach Rupp held up his closed fist with his thumb sticking up, showing how *fierce* a fighter he was, then said, "Oh, I gave him a mighty blow."

One day early in the season my parents came to Lexington to go to a game with me. We were standing in front of the Phoenix Hotel when I saw Coach Rupp walking down the street. I stepped out toward him and called, "Hey, Coach, I want you to meet my parents!" He never even looked at me. He heard me, for sure, but he ignored me and kept on walking. My parents laughingly asked, "Joe, are you sure you know him?" That incident proved that if he had very little to say to me on the floor, he had nothing to say to me off the floor.

13

The Fabulous Five

Never let your head hang down. Never give up and sit down
and grieve. Find another way. And don't pray when it rains if
you don't pray when the sun shines.

Leroy "Satchel" Paige

I attended UK from the fall of 1947 to the end of 1948—the best
and the worst of times. It was the best of times to learn from a
great coach, but it was the worst of times to get a chance to play
ball. The competition that year was terrific. The Wildcats had an
abundance of great athletes. Many of them were veterans, returning
as sophomores, juniors, or seniors to complete their degrees. They
were all mature men. I was the only kid on the squad.

Three of the veterans were so outstanding they were part of
a team, called the Fabulous Five, that was unstoppable. They were
Alex Groza, center; Cliff Barker, forward; and Kenny Rollins, guard.
Their military experience had made them big and strong. The other
two were nonveterans—Ralph Beard, guard, and Wallace "Wah
Wah" Jones, forward. They were All-Americans in high school.
The Fabulous Five won the University of Kentucky's first NCAA
Men's Basketball championships in 1948, and they won again in
1949. They won the National Invitational Tournament (NIT)
championship in 1946 and four Southeastern Conference (SEC)
championships. Moreover, they were part of the US Olympic team
that won gold medals in 1948 in London. I did not get to attend
that great event.

The oldest member of the team was Barker at twenty-seven,
then Rollins, about twenty-five, and Groza, who was only twenty-

two but acted much older. These men had unbelievable skills that they had developed from being in the military. And there I was—a skinny kid who didn't even need to shave every day. But I was a kid with lots of determination. I had some confidence too.

One time, in practice, Coach Rupp had me playing defense on drills, and I was blocking everybody's layups. I must have blocked ten layups in a row. Nobody could score. Then he called Jack Parkinson, a former All-American, also a veteran and a senior, to come to him. He whispered something in Jack's ear. The next time Jack went through the drill, he unexpectedly ducked. When I went up to block his shot, he flipped me in the air, and I fell on the floor in the Alumni Gym from way up. Ouch! That hurt! Other players ran over to help me up and asked if I were all right. Not a one of them tried to conceal his disapproval of what Coach Rupp and Jack did to me. I didn't know what to think until another player whispered to me, "Guess the old man got tired of watching you block too many from scoring."

The star players were fascinating to watch. Cliff Barker had been a prisoner in Germany for over a year before he was rescued by Patton's Third Army. While he was a POW, he sometimes got a little chance to practice basketball with a volleyball. Of course, you can do things with a volleyball in passing and shooting that you can't do with a basketball because it's larger. Whenever he had a little time, he practiced and gradually developed skills of ball handling, passing, and shooting that no one else at that time around here had. With his sleight-of hand, he could take the ball behind his back, bounce pass it between his legs, throw it behind his back, look one way and throw the ball another way. He dazzled you with his ball-handling skills.

Barker was also crafty and tough. Although he never talked about his wartime experiences with us, we were told that when his B-17 bomber was shot down over Germany, a farmer working in the field saw him fall and ran up to where he was lying. His package of cigarettes was lying near him. The farmer snatched the package and started running. Cliff got up, ran after him, grabbed him, and snatched the cigarettes out of the farmer's hand. Then he took one cigarette out and handed it to the farmer, who quickly ran off.

After all the terrible experiences he had endured in the war, Cliff was not about to put up with anyone bothering him, including Coach Rupp. I remember well how he'd laugh or scoff when Coach Rupp yelled at him. Sometimes during the middle of scrimmaging, he just sat down and took off one of his shoes and rested. The first time he did that, Coach Rupp shouted, "Cliff, what the hell are you doing? Get up!" Cliff shouted back, "My feet are burning!" and continued to rest. After that, he sat on the floor and rested whenever he needed to and Coach Rupp never again said anything about it.

I will never forget the first time I guarded Ralph Beard. He was only a year ahead of me but seemed much older. I was nervous, yes, but I had some confidence in my ability and knew I was a pretty good defensive man. I could shut out a lot of people, but I quickly learned that Ralph Beard was not one of them. The first time I guarded him in practice, I got down in front of him, got my hands down low, spread out wide, and looked him in the eye—while he bounced the ball between my legs to Groza and, before I could even get straightened up, was already running past me going in for a layup. That experience was a real wake-up call. When Beard guarded me in practice, he challenged me every time. He was so quick, so aggressive, so tenacious, and so competitive. He was an outstanding shooter too. One time I stole the ball from him and was beating him down the court when he tripped and fell. Yet he still blocked my shot. I mean, he didn't lose a second in falling. He was great! I can't say enough good things about him. He was just an all-around great athlete and a nice guy. If he were playing today he'd be an All-American.

Kenny Rollins had served in the navy. He was a great defensive man, very fast, and one of the most unselfish players I have ever known. He was an intelligent, gifted man with an even temperament,

47

always calm no matter what the circumstances. Whenever the rest of us were upset because we had been chewed out or left out, Kenny could settle us down. Yes, Kenny was a calming influence and a very good man. I admired and respected him.

We had a lot of excitement the night of December 16, 1948, when we played Holy Cross in Boston Gardens. Wah had been playing on the football team and went straight to basketball before he had a chance to improve his basketball skills. That night he just did not have the finesse yet that he needed, so he ended up with five fouls. Also, Wah was very strong; in fact, a few of his opponents complained he'd hurt them—left them bruised.

That night the Boston fans, known for being rowdy, heckled us all throughout the game. Some of them were sitting nearby, behind us. I kept looking back at them, watching one who had been yelling at Wah, calling him "Yellow!" and shouting things like "Take your shoes off, you big dumb hillbilly!" The crowd went wild—I mean really crazy wild—when the game ended with us winning 51–48.

As we were standing up, putting on our warm-ups and getting ready to walk off the floor, I glanced back at that guy who had been yelling at Wah. I watched him wad up a wet empty cigarette package and throw it, hitting Wah in the corner of his eye. With his long powerful arms and legs, Wah leaped over those bleachers, grabbed that guy, and hit him so hard he made him the first man ever to go into outer space. Then the hecklers began descending upon us. Harry sprang into action, pulling one guy's shirt off and then hitting him so hard he passed out. We picked up a bench and rammed the crowd to keep it from crushing us. I saw Coach Rupp almost fall after getting shoved and punched. It was bedlam! It was terrible! Police and ushers ran to our rescue and led us out to our hotel.

On December 18 we played St. John's in Madison Square Garden. We beat them 57–30. Coach always played seven or eight players although he had a twelve-man squad. That night he played seven only. None of us subs—Garland Townes, John Stough,

Robert Henne, and me—minded not getting to play in the Holy Cross game because it was so close—51–48. But at Madison Square Garden we won over St. Johns by twenty-seven points. Coach Rupp could easily have let us all play, but he chose not to. We were so disappointed we could have cried. And so we called his team the Fabulous Five and the rest of us the Sorry Seven.

Why didn't he let us play? We had practiced hard and done all that he had asked of us. To play in Madison Square Garden— the mecca of basketball in the United States, for both pro and college, was a dream every one of us on the bench had. Coach Rupp knew that; he had to know that. For a young lad from Cynthiana, Kentucky, to be at Madison Square Garden and not be in the game was heartbreaking. It was an experience I have never forgotten. It was what led me in the 1978 championship game against Duke to empty my bench and play every sub—including walk-ons (nonscholarship players). Only when Duke narrowed our margin did I reinsert our starters.

We began the 1948–1949 season without Kenny Rollins, who had graduated. Coach Rupp replaced him with Dale Barnstable, who had been the sixth man on the Fabulous Five the previous season. I was the only one from the freshman class he selected to be on the squad. From the sophomore class, he chose Walter Hirsch, Bob Henne, Roger Day, and Garland Townes.

Still, I was sitting so far down the bench that if Coach Rupp wanted me he would have had to get an usher to find me. I wanted to play. To understand the excitement of being on that floor with other Wildcats, you'd have to be like me—a born Kentuckian who loved Kentucky, loved basketball, and loved the University of Kentucky Wildcats. It was thrilling for me to run onto that floor, dressed in my uniform, number 31, with *Kentucky* spelled out in big blue letters, while the band played our fight song, "On, On, U of K, On!" My dream, of course, was to throw the ball, watch it sail through the air, drop smoothly down into the basket, and listen to the crowd cheer—sadly enough, that did not happen.

Coach Rupp let me play in three of the first four games in 1948. We beat Indiana Central 74–38, De Paul 67–36, Tulsa 81–27, and Arkansas 76–39. In the Arkansas game I stole the ball at mid-court and went in for a left-hand layup. Not trusting my left hand, I crossed over and made a right-hand layup that rolled around the rim twice and fell off. I felt awful. That night I felt like I deserved every one of the terrible names Coach Rupp had ever called me in practice.

When he chose Dale Barnstable to be his varsity guard—a position I had hoped to get—I knew that I would never be playing. I had not contributed anything to the team so far, and it was apparent that I was not going to get a chance to do so in future. I was discouraged and sad.

14

Sewanee

Getting over a painful experience is much like crossing monkey bars. You have to let go at some point in order to move forward.

C. S. Lewis

The four of us subs cheered up thinking and talking about going to New Orleans to play in the Sugar Bowl. I had never been to the Big Easy, where there is supposed to be a relaxed and easygoing way of life. I was looking forward to seeing the city. Then one afternoon right after Christmas, Coach Rupp called the four of us into his office. He said he had decided to take only ten boys to New Orleans with him, and he wanted us to draw straws to see which two of us would make the trip. Draw straws? What a surprise. I did not like that idea at all. I said, "No thanks, Coach," and walked out.

The next day I told him I wanted to transfer to another school where I could play ball. I asked if he would help me, and he said he would. He understood my desire but didn't offer me any hope to play ball for him. The next morning, he told me that I could get a full scholarship and earn $100 a month with a work-study program at Xavier. He also said Duke was trying to improve its program, and I could go there. All of that sounded awfully good.

A night or so later, I was lying on my bed in my dorm room listening to a sports radio program broadcast out of Louisville. Coach Lon Varnell of Sewanee—the University of the South—was being interviewed. He said he had been told that Kentucky had plenty of good guards, and he was here looking for one who could play for him immediately. Sewanee was not a Division One school, so it did not have to follow the NCAA regulation forbidding transfer students from playing ball their first year. I made up my mind right then that that was where I wanted to go. I didn't even know where it was located.

The next day I told Coach Rupp about the radio interview. I knew he and Varnell were friends, and I asked if he would call him on my behalf. He said sure and pointed out another fact in my favor: Varnell had spent a year observing the Kentucky program, and he ran the same offense, so it would be very easy for me to make the adjustment. Within just a few hours, I received a phone call from the Sewanee coach telling me, "Hey, Joe. Come on down!" I left UK on very good terms with Coach Rupp. He knew I appreciated his help.

Arrangements were made for Sewanee players Bob Ward, from Georgetown, and Bob Logan, from Shelbyville, who were home for the holidays, to take me to Sewanee. The date and time for us to leave was set, and I was ready to go. In addition to being late picking me up, which annoyed me, the guys said they were going to make a stop in Bowling Green where they had dates with sorority girls. Trying to make me feel better, they said they had a date for me too. It was clear to me that they were not as eager as I was to get to my destination. I kept asking how long it would take us to get there, but they never would say. Finally I had to admit that I did not even know which state the school was in.

That morning when we pulled into the entrance of Sewanee's campus, I was stunned by the sheer beauty of the place—the trees, shrubs, buildings, and natural landscaping looked beautiful. It is built on top of the Cumberland Plateau in Tennessee. Its Gothic-style buildings are all made of stones carved from the mountains and patterned after the old universities in England. I learned the institution was founded in the late 1850s by some Episcopalians who started it as an all-male college and a seminary for those who wanted to be priests. When I was there in 1949, it was still a college for men only. However, Sewanee opened its enrollment to women in the 1960s. What surprised and impressed me the most was that all facets of life there were based on the honor system: "I will not lie, steal, or cheat." If you caught someone doing any of those things, according to school policy you should not fail to report it. Just like every other student enrolling there, I had to sign a paper agreeing that I would abide by the code.

Sewanee was unlike UK or any other college that I had seen— not only in appearance but in its traditions. When I asked why some men walking around campus were dressed in long black gowns, I was told they were members of the Order of the Gownsmen, an academic honor society. The order's members were upperclassmen who had B averages or above, exhibited high moral standards, and led exemplary lives. They were given certain privileges, such as skipping classes without penalties. They could also take tests wherever they wanted—in their dorm rooms, the library, on the lawn, or wherever they chose. The professors were all highly educated scholars, with doctorates from prestigious universities. All the classes were small. My economics class had only twelve students. The professor was Dr. Cayden, who was President Roosevelt's economic adviser. All the faculty, and some were priests, were members of Phi Beta Kappa (an elite honor society). They also were kind and helpful. They showed a genuine interest in each student's progress. My adviser was my English teacher, whom I admired. In fact, I appreciated everyone I met there.

I practiced all week with the team before I registered because I wasn't sure I was going to stay. Coach Varnell told me, "Joe, tomorrow is the last day to enroll. You have got to enroll if you want play in the first home game Saturday. It's against Birmingham Southern. They beat us the last time we played them." I did enroll and we did win the game; I scored eleven points in it. In the next game I scored nineteen points against Cumberland Tennessee at Cumberland. Then in the third game, I set the scoring record for Sewanee with twenty-six points against Millsap's in Mississippi. We won that game too. I played well in all the games and my coach let me know he was proud of me. For the first time in a long time, I felt good about myself. He and I remained friends until the end of his life.

A few years later, when I returned to UK, Coach Lancaster asked me why I didn't score at UK like I did at Sewanee, and I asked him, "Coach, who guarded me at UK?" He chuckled and said, "Oh, yeah. Beard."

I did not have a minute of spare time at Sewanee. I'd go to class, then to practice, then I'd go about my various jobs, and then study. Along with five other boys, I lived in Coach Varnell's house. We were given the three upstairs bedrooms for our quarters and were expected to keep ourselves and our space clean. We all worked at various little jobs.

To earn as much as I could, I had four jobs. After practice every day, I was responsible for driving Coach Varnell's two little boys on their evening paper route, and I had to get us home in time for supper. On Sundays we delivered the morning paper, so we had to get up early to pick up the papers, fold them, and go on our route.

Also, each day I would buy a crate of seventy-two apples for $4. I would usually get red delicious if they were available. Then I would fill some small boxes with the apples, which I sold for 10 cents each. I would drive around to each dorm and leave a box of apples by the entrance. Every morning I would collect the empty boxes and the change. One morning, one box was short a dime, but the next morning that same box had an extra dime, proving that the honor system worked.

My third job was with a laundry service downtown, which hired me to collect bags of soiled clothes and deliver cleaned ones. I would leave a laundry bag in the big closet in the entry hall of each dorm for students to deposit their dirty clothes. In those days we wore coats and ties to classes. Many of our clothes had to be dry-cleaned. There was no such thing as wash and wear or wrinkle free then. Each day I would go into town to pick up the clean laundry and hang the pieces in the closets of the individual dorms for their owners to pick up.

My fourth job was managing the popcorn machine at the theater. In addition, I hired a boy to sell boxes of popcorn at football games and beer parties for me.

I managed all these jobs while still attending basketball practice every afternoon. I remember having a terrible time with shin splints and had to miss practice sometimes.

Before the semester ended Coach Varnell talked to me about going with him and seven other basketball players on an overseas tour he was going to make that summer for the US State Department. I gladly accepted his invitation.

15

My World Tour

Broad, wholesome, charitable views of men and things cannot be acquired by vegetating in one little corner of the earth all of one's lifetime.

Mark Twain

In the summer of 1951, I went with Coach Varnell and his collegiate all-star team to tour Europe and Africa. Our team was sponsored by the US State Department at the invitation of the Amateur Basketball Federation of Europe. It was a goodwill tour, and we would be a preliminary attraction for the Harlem Globetrotters. Coach Varnell was a promoter for that popular team.

That tour was a remarkable experience but very tiring. We played fifty-six games in fifty-eight days; we won fifty-four of those games—the last thirty-five consecutively. We had only two days off. We traveled in fourteen different countries in Europe and in Africa for two months, playing national teams before the Harlem Globetrotters entertained everyone.

One night in Naples, we played the Italian national team, whose members were so convinced they would be the winners they already had their name engraved on the trophy. They got to keep that trophy too. They beat us. Later, when we played them again in Geneva in the championship game in the International Tournament, we beat them. We also beat the teams from Spain and Switzerland in the international tournaments.

Traveling through different countries was exciting and educational. The thrill of playing different teams every night was exhilarating. Trying to communicate with people whose languages we could not speak was a real challenge, but we managed well. We visited places I had heard of all my life, and some I did not even know existed. We enjoyed every bit of what we were seeing, learning, and doing, and we played a great every game every night. It was a happy, memorable experience for this kid from Cynthiana, Kentucky.

Our tour ended one month early and abruptly when the US State Department told us to come home. Our government was concerned about the increasingly dangerous anti-American feelings in Europe.

Just a few days before Coach Varnell received the telegram from the State Department, Sugar Ray Robinson, the boxing champ, had been bombarded by angry German protestors throwing pop bottles at him while he was in the ring. Security guards had to rush him to safety underneath the ring.

The highlight of the entire tour for me was meeting Jesse Owens. Just fifteen years earlier, he had won four gold medals in the 1936 Summer Olympics in Berlin and set three world records. Just as we were doing, he was traveling with the Globetrotters, going back to Berlin to hold track clinics and to race against horses. I made a point of sitting next to him on the bus every chance I got. We became friends and stayed in touch. A few years later, when I was back at the University of Kentucky finishing work on my degree, I invited him to come to Lexington to speak at our annual track meet banquet. He accepted my invitation and was a tremendous hit with the crowd that night. Everyone loved him. Jesse was a great person. He was warm, friendly, and modest, and he is still the greatest the world has known in track and field.

Jesse said that there were seventeen other black American athletes in the 1936 Summer Olympics and many of them won gold, silver, or bronze medals. The thing about their winning that made it so sweet was Hitler had held the Olympics in Berlin in the first place to show off his "superior race"—the Aryans, white people from northern Europe, especially Germany. He believed his people were far superior to other races, and he expected to prove his belief to the entire world at the Olympics. Jesse's victory, along with those of the other American black medalists, proved to the world just how foolishly mistaken the Führer was. The German runner competing with Jesse in the first hundred-yard dash came in fifth place.

My favorite story of his had to do with his German competitor, "Luz" Long, a long jumper who actually helped him win the gold. Luz, he said, was an example of Hitler's ideal man—tall, blond, blue-eyed, and very handsome. He was also a good man. Before they were about to compete in the long jump, Jesse said, they shook hands and wished each other good luck. In the qualifying phase, according to Jesse, each athlete had three tries, and he got panicky after he missed his first two. He said Luz calmed him down by showing him where he was making his mistake: he was going way past the lift-off line to jump. Luz advised him to place a marker of some kind, like a towel or stick, about a foot back of the lift-off line so he would know exactly where to place his foot to start. Jesse did that and won the gold medal. He broke the Olympic record by jumping twenty-six feet, five inches, and won four gold medals in track and field events. He and Luz continued to be friends and corresponded until Luz was killed in action in World War II. Jesse said that after that he reached out to Luz's son. It is not unusual for some athletes to develop strong, lasting friendships with their competitors as well as their teammates.

While we were still touring, we watched Jesse perform some astonishing half-time exhibitions at Globetrotters games. He was such a smooth runner, never looked as if he was pushing himself. He was amazing. It was hard to believe that he was actually doing the things we saw him do. He ran the hurdles around chairs while carrying a cup and saucer and never moved his head or dropped the dishes. He had total mind control. The secret to his success, he said, was determination and total concentration on what you have to do.

I learned so much from him about training for competition and about my own country. He made me think about racial issues here in the United States, a subject I had never heard anyone talk about before. He was so interesting, so knowledgeable about current affairs. What he had to say about how blacks were treated (mistreated is a better word) here in the US stayed with me. I didn't grow up among people who drew such distinctions between the races. The black people in Cynthiana were all, to my knowledge, good, hardworking, respectable people. They were bricklayers, carpenters, painters, gardeners, plumbers, wallpaper hangers, storekeepers. In other words, they were respected businesspeople. My dad was a postal worker for many years, and he delivered mail to many black families. He knew all of them well. As a result, I knew many of them too: I grew up playing with their children and we all remained friends as adults. Later, after Dad was elected sheriff, he never had any problems with them either. But then Cynthiana was a peaceful little town.

Although he had received a good bit of attention from the American public after he returned in 1936, Jesse did not get what he should have received. The reason was, he pointed out, that nothing in the States had changed—segregation still prevailed. It was obvious that after fifteen years, he was still disappointed that President Roosevelt had ignored him, never invited him to the White House to shake his hand, never sent him a congratulatory telegram or letter. Mrs. Roosevelt, who claimed to be such an advocate for the underprivileged, never contacted him either. Yet they recognized all the white athletes.

Many years later, I remember reading about President Gerald Ford praising Jesse. When Jesse, only sixty-six, died in 1980, President Carter paid a great tribute to him. Even later still, President Obama and Mrs. Obama honored all the families of the black 1936 Summer Olympic athletes at the White House. Guess that's what we can call a little too late—but better late than never, I suppose.

After we got home from the tour, I returned to Sewanee. During the Christmas holidays, I became very ill with pleurisy and was taken home. After I recovered, I did not return to Sewanee.

I was still tired from the tour and burned out with school. I was not sure I wanted a career in law or in the ministry. I didn't really know what I wanted to do. My dad, of course, urged me to get a job. A friend of his had just retired from H. J. Heinz Company, where he made a good living, so Dad knew there was an opening that I could possibly get. That's how I became a Heinz salesman, peddling canned foods, catsup, and pickles to cafes, restaurants, and school cafeterias throughout our neighboring counties. I have always enjoyed talking to people, and persuading them to buy my products, which were tasty, was easy. But I knew for certain that I did not want to do that kind of work the rest of my life.

16

Katharine

Doubt thou the stars are fire;
Doubt that the sun doth move;
Doubt truth to be a liar;
But never doubt I love.

Shakespeare

One day while I was on my daily Heinz route, a kitchen worker in a Butler elementary school told me that one of the school's young teachers was from my home county and that I ought to stay for the noon break to meet her. I did just that, and found that I already knew her—slightly. She was Katharine Dennis—someone I had admired "from afar," as they say, for a long time. She was a little younger than I and from Berry, near Cynthiana. I had seen her about town. She was well known in our area for her lovely voice; she sang at weddings, parties, funerals, and church services. She had attended UK while I was there, and I would search for her on campus and walk with her to class. I could not afford to invite her for a date then. Now that I had a job and had found her again, I asked her to go to dinner that very night. She accepted.

To give you an idea of just how beautiful she was, she was crowned Miss Kentucky at the state fair that summer of 1951 and was the runner-up in the National Rural Electric Cooperative Corporation Fair the same year. For her talent presentations in the contests, she sang. She could have easily had a professional career, but she never desired or attempted to do so. She said she wanted to be a wife and a mother.

On our first date, I drove her in my new 1951 blue, four-door Plymouth to what was then rated the finest restaurant in Cincinnati—the Maisonette. One of my relatives knew the owner, so we may have been given a little extra special service. Katharine and I knew that night, on our first date, that we were meant for each other and we wanted to be together always.

Neither one of us wanted a big wedding, so six weeks later, on the morning of Saturday, October 27, 1951, two days after Katharine's twentieth birthday, I picked her up from her apartment in Butler, and we drove to Lexington, where we were married in the chapel of the Porter Memorial Baptist Church by its pastor. My brother Bill was my best man. Jo Shropshire Hill (the wife of one of my best buddies) was Katharine's bridesmaid. We left right after the short ceremony and drove straight to Sewanee, Tennessee, where I had made reservations for us at the Sewanee Inn. It was a lovely place, and guests were mostly parents visiting their children, students at Sewanee. That college campus built on top of the Cumberland Plateau is an unforgettable, beautiful, peaceful place. And that fall day, it was especially beautiful. We spent one night there and left early Sunday morning for home.

First, we went straight to her parents' house in Berry and told them what we had done. As we suspected, her mother was upset at first, and understandably so. Having four sons and only one daughter, Mrs. Dennis had always dreamed of seeing her daughter in a beautiful veil and bridal gown, and of her having a big, beautiful wedding and reception. When she learned that we had eloped, she was visibly disappointed, especially with me—but just for a little while. She had gotten to know me pretty well because I was at their house so often. Katharine invited me to their Sunday dinners, and I was frequently there during the week also. After nearly six weeks of my courting her daughter, Mrs. Dennis knew me, and she knew that Katharine and I were seriously in love. Because she liked and trusted me, and saw how happy we were together, she quickly forgave us.

That same Sunday evening, we drove back to Cynthiana

and moved some of our things into our first home—a little guest cottage that I had rented from friends John and Sara McGarvey. We commuted to our jobs.

Now that I had a wife, I asked Heinz for a raise, or a better paying position, but was turned down. They said they were too pleased with the success I was having with my present job to promote me. If they gave me a raise, they would also have to give one to the other salesman, who had been with them for years, and they were not going to do that. I knew I had no future with that company, so I resigned and talked to Katharine about what I really wanted to do. I told her I wanted to finish my degree and find a coaching job in a college or university. She agreed and said in the meantime we would get by on her salary and with whatever I could make doing part-time work. She said we would be fine!

I completed my studies at the University of Kentucky and received my degree in January 1955, the same year our first child, Judy, was born. All the coaching jobs had been taken by that time, so I went to work as a production scheduler with Kawneer Aluminum Manufacturing in Cynthiana. I had an office and a secretary but a low salary. When I asked to transfer to sales, where I could earn more, I was told they couldn't move me because they had trained me to do the job I was doing and, no, they were not giving me a raise.

The only thing I loved about working for Kawneer was coaching my little baseball team (sponsored by the company) in the summer. I had a great little team and those little boys worked so hard, doing everything I asked them to do. When the season ended, we were undefeated. After that experience, I knew for certain I wanted a career in coaching college basketball. I asked Katharine if she would allow me ten years to see if I could succeed in coaching. I promised her that if after those ten years I had failed, then I would find another kind of work to support us. She agreed that I should pursue my dream. I went directly to the placement office at UK and inquired about coaching jobs. It was August by then and all the jobs had been taken except one, the clerk said. I told her that I would take it before I even asked where it was. As it turned out, it was a small high school in Shepherdsville, Kentucky, a little town along the Salt River in Bullitt County, south of Louisville (more on the place and the job in the next chapter).

Our second baby was due to be born later that same month—August—so Katharine and I rented a little house in Shepherdsville. The plan was that as her due date drew closer, I would take Katharine to her mother's so she could have the baby at the Cynthiana hospital. We knew she would be far better off with her mother and her obstetrician. I would come as soon as I got word.

Our first tour of the high school was extremely disappointing. It was so run-down and dreary. It needed obvious repairs and a good cleaning and painting. The locker rooms were disgraceful, and the gym floor needed sanding and refinishing. The football field, too, was in terrible shape. Parts of it were in a low area and needed dirt hauled in to fill holes. All of this work had to be done in less than two weeks, so I got busy—working day and night—repairing, cleaning, painting, filling holes in the football field, and refinishing the gym floor.

The night Katharine went into labor—earlier than expected—and was taken to the hospital, her mother was unable to reach me because I was frantically trying to finish the gym floor and did not hear the one phone in the entire building ring. Cell phones did not exist then. No one else was in the building that late at night, and the only telephone was in the principal's office. At dawn the next morning, a call awakened me saying I was the father of another little girl. I dressed hurriedly and left for Cynthiana to see my wife and new daughter.

Katharine was an ideal coach's wife—and it's no easy job. After I became coach at UK and the children were a little older, she went with me to games and other sporting events as often as she could. She never got upset when I brought unexpected guests home for supper or when I brought a sick boy home, as I often did, for her to nurse back to health. She didn't mind when the boys would stop by our house without prior notice for a meal, just to visit, or to ask for help with a problem.

At Christmas, Thanksgiving, and all other holidays, she always cooked huge meals for the players who lived out of town. They did not have enough time to travel to their own homes and return in time for practice sessions that went on during the holidays. She made certain those boys had a grand holiday meal with all the trimmings. Katharine never complained about having the major responsibility of caring for the children and the house, although I know now how problematic those things can be sometimes. Later, after we moved to Lexington, I was often away—recruiting, attending out-of-town games, or working late in my office—but I tried my hardest never to be away from home two consecutive nights.

Coming from a farming family, Katharine knew how to manage money, the house, and the children. She grew up in a loving family and in a good environment. She was thrifty but not stingy. She was resourceful. When recruits visited UK, I would always take them and my family out to dinner at a fine restaurant in Lexington. Usually the meal would be the same: big ribeye or sirloin steaks, twice-baked potatoes, salad, iced tea, and dessert.

One night at one of our favorite steak houses, we had been waiting far too long for our meals to be served. We had three small children by then—Judy, Kathy, and Steve—all of whom were tired and hungry. I was not sure what to do. The owner finally called me aside, apologizing, and explained that his chef had gotten into a fight with other workers in the kitchen and most of them had walked out. The two who stayed were doing their best to get the earlier orders out. Katharine told me, "Let me go see what I can do." She rose from her chair and walked into the kitchen. Less than thirty minutes later, she reappeared carrying a platter of sandwiches she had made using roasted turkey breast and freshly baked bread. The kitchen worker followed her with extra pickles, lettuce, tomatoes, onions, and even desserts. Katharine had saved the day—again!

For years during the Christmas holidays, we'd have a big open-house party. My friend Herb Burstein, a builder in New Orleans and a friend of the Robey family (Rick Robey was one of the "twin towers" on the Wildcats team), would fly into Lexington on the morning of the party with tubs of iced-down shrimp, oysters, and crabs. We would serve all that seafood on top of trays covered in ice.

Katharine and the girls, with Steve's help, would be busy days in advance decorating the house for the holiday and making all kinds of delicious treats and sweets. I think everyone had a great time at those parties. She and the children worked hard getting ready for those events and then cleaning up afterward.

17

Shepherdsville

If one advances confidently in the direction of his dreams, and endeavors to live the life he has imagined, he will meet with a success in uncommon hours.

Henry David Thoreau

In advancing toward my dreams of someday having a great coaching career, I started out by taking a cut in salary to coach at Shepherdsville, a small high school in a little rural area in Kentucky that hired me to teach classes in health and physical education and to coach baseball, basketball, and, much to my surprise, also football. After the football coach got drafted into the army just days before school started, coaching football was added to my responsibilities. I was not prepared to coach football, and our first game with Elizabethtown, a much larger and finer school, had been scheduled in one week. I had exactly one week to prepare my boys, who were all so young, optimistic, and cooperative. They had only played six-man football, but we had an eleven-man team.

At that first game, I made my first coaching mistake: I sent my players out on the field first. All nineteen of them—pencil-necked kids, looking small and frightened as we silently watched Elizabethtown's big band come marching out, proudly playing their school song to much applause. The band was followed by the football players running out of the locker room one by one and circling the entire field. All 108 of them stood straight and still, looking strong, as they absorbed the crowd's cheers. We sighed and silently watched, feeling like Custer at the battle of Little Big Horn. Alas, we did not win that game. In fact, we did not win a game all that season—but we tied one.

My best basketball player at Shepherdsville was James Ray Jones, an African American boy who integrated as a junior the first year I was there. He was six foot six and had played little basketball, though he seemed a natural for the game. After I started working with him, I noticed he could shoot, but he could not vertical jump very well. I was determined to help him. I built and attached a weightlifting apparatus onto the end of my taping table and had him sit on the end of the table and lift the device (it was on hinges) up and down multiple times. He did this exercise and others daily along with the other players using equipment we had made ourselves with plumbing pipes for barbells. By the time basketball season started, they were all stronger, and James Ray could jump with ease some eight inches higher. He ended up scoring as many as twenty-four points in a game.

That experience was the second proof I had of the value of a conditioning and strengthening program. I knew how much good such exercises, in addition to the hard work I did in the summers on my uncle's farm, had done for me. I was always much stronger and had more endurance than many other boys my age. From then on, I knew that wherever I coached I would begin each year with a conditioning program.

I have never forgotten those kids at Shepherdsville. I loved them, and they loved me. When they learned I was leaving after my second year, they begged me to stay and even produced a petition to keep me there. I think just about everybody in the school and the town signed it. It was a very moving experience. The 1957 school yearbook included this tribute to the football team and me: "Although the team did not win any games this year, it showed fine possibilities for the future. Coach Hall needs to be congratulated for the fine job he did with the team, since this is Rams' first year of eleven-man football. The scores do not reflect the fine play and the sportsmanship of the team."

We did better in basketball, and we had lots of supporters. Although our old gym seated only eight hundred, more than a thousand spectators crowded in—and many of them smoked! Back then, so many people smoked and smoked in the gym. I don't know how we stood it. Our season ended with a 22–6 record. We went to the Eighth Regional finals, where we lost to Shelbyville 84–77. I was named conference coach of the year, and a very nice article appeared in the county newspaper about how well behaved our boys were, what gentlemen all sixteen of them were.

18

Regis College

Basketball is a beautiful game when the five players on the
court play with one heartbeat.

Dean Smith

In 1959, Katharine was far along in her pregnancy with our third
child, our son Steve, so the long car drive, pulling a U-Haul
trailer loaded with all our worldly possessions, from Shepherdsville
to Denver, Colorado, could not have been easy for her, yet she did
not complain. I stopped often for her to rest, and for the girls to run
around a bit.

Regis was a step up for me, with a little better pay. I was hired
as an assistant basketball coach and a physical education instructor.
The next year the head coach moved away, and I was selected from
among the thirty-three other applicants to replace him. A small
Jesuit college, Regis operated on a tight budget. It would hire one
person to do several jobs. Although my contract said I was to coach
basketball and baseball and teach physical education classes, I was
also responsible for managing the swimming pool, which included
keeping the pool clean, teaching swimming lessons, and training
lifeguards. After a while, serving as athletic director was added
to my list of responsibilities. With that schedule, I still managed
to earn my master's degree at nearby Northern Colorado State
College during the six years I was at Regis.

The first week on the job, I put in a running and weightlifting
program. I had to make some adjustments because of Denver's
mile-high elevation. In such an environment, with less oxygen, I
had the boys eat foods high in potassium and drink lots of water. I

gradually built their endurance and strength. They became superbly conditioned with running and weightlifting. They ran cross-country and sprints. While many of the teams that came to Denver to play us would fade in the second half, my team remained strong. The conditioning program was very successful. Over the years I coached at Regis, we beat some top schools: Arizona, Denver, Colorado State, Oklahoma State, Oklahoma City, and the Air Force Academy. Though a very small college, Regis was rated as a major college in basketball. Regis was an all-boy school with 650 students enrolled. We had to apply to the NCAA for major college status, and we were approved because of the strength of our schedule.

When we beat Oklahoma State—fourth in the nation—I had conflicted feelings of happiness and regret. I had and have now so much respect and admiration for Coach Henry Iba that I hated to beat his great team, yet I was also thrilled to do so. To show you what kind of man he was, immediately after the game, as the students were lifting me up on their shoulders, Coach Iba was the first to reach up and shake my hand to congratulate me. I'll never forget hearing that raspy voice of his telling me how proud he was of me. Mr. Iba was the dean of cage coaches and a prince of a man. By then he had won two NCAA Division One championships back to back, 1946 and 1947. He went on to receive many other great honors.

He was so highly regarded as a person that his players and nearly everyone else called him Mr. Iba, not Coach Iba. He is the only coach I ever heard of who was honored that way. I learned so much by observing him, and I don't just mean his great defensive basketball strategies. I mean the way he interacted with people. He treated everyone with respect. He was as friendly with busboys, waiters, ushers, and managers as he was with the owners and authorities.

That night I received a telegram from Coach Rupp congratulating me, saying how proud he was of me and my team. It was great hearing from him again. He had sent me a note once before asking me to meet with him when he was in Cynthiana to give a talk, but I was sick then and unable to attend. I appreciated his effort to maintain our relationship, and as often as I could I recommended players to him.

The boy I had helped to learn to jump higher, James Ray Jones from Shepherdsville, followed me to Regis. Then I recruited Louis Stout from Cynthiana. High school principal Kelly Stanfield wrote a letter on Louis's behalf, and the whole community backed his going to Denver. He received a scholarship and made good use of it too. Louis was a great asset to our team and to our student body athletically and academically. He was handsome and a gentleman. He did really well in his studies and earned his bachelor's degree. My wife and I remained friends with those two boys. They were in our home often and ate many meals with us. We thought so much of them that we used them as babysitters occasionally.

Louis, I am proud to say, went on to have a splendid career in basketball, winning many honors. He was the first African American in the nation to be named commissioner of the Kentucky High School Athletic Association.

19

Great Opportunity

Life was always about waiting for the right moment to act.

Paulo Coelho

While I was head coach at Regis, Coach Rupp phoned me in my office one early summer afternoon asking if I would come to UK as his recruiter. I told him I loved coaching too much and did not want to be a recruiter, but if he ever needed a floor coach, I would jump at that opportunity. I needed experience as an assistant coach at a major college if I were ever going to get ahead. I planned to wait for such an opportunity.

I stayed at Regis for six years and then accepted what I thought would be a better job at Central Missouri, where there was a track that I could use for my conditioning program. The conditioning program was very successful. Our team won the Christmas Tournament, the MIAA Tournament, and the MIAA Conference championship. I was selected MIAA Conference coach of the year.

In the late summer of 1965, I attended a summer basketball clinic in St. Louis where Coach Rupp was the speaker. He recognized me and introduced me to the audience, saying many nice things about me. After he finished his talk and was leaving the podium, he beckoned me to him, indicating he wanted to talk to me. Once we were seated in his room, he asked if I would come to UK—as his *first assistant coach!* Puzzled, I asked, "First assistant?" "Yes," he replied. I could hardly believe what I was hearing.

Harry Lancaster had been his first assistant since 1946, but they had known each other before that. They worked well together. Everyone in the program figured Harry was his most likely successor—and rightfully so. I asked him, "What's happened to Harry? Is Harry leaving?" He said, "No, he is still here, but he has been leaving me in the spring after basketball season to coach baseball and is not available anymore to help me with the spring recruiting." He added, "I need someone here to help me all year! Someone who knows the program. That's why I want you to be my No. 1 assistant and to share recruiting." This was such astonishingly good news that I could hardly believe it! I said, "I'm on! I will be there." I was so happy! And I knew Katharine and the children would be thrilled to return home to Kentucky. As I turned the lights out in my office that evening and closed the door, I whispered, "Thank you, God," and headed home to my family. Soon after that, I went to Lexington to firm up the details of my move.

Near the end of May 1965, I met with the University of Kentucky athletic director Bernie Shively and Coach Rupp to sign my contract, which stated that I was hired as Coach Rupp's No. 1 assistant and one of the three recruiters.

A few days later, my wife and children joined me in Lexington. On Katharine's first evening in town, Coach Rupp and Esther, his wife, took us to dinner at the Tates' Creek Country Club. After we had been seated for a few minutes, he beckoned a man standing across the room to come over to our table. He said to me, "This is someone I want you to meet. Joe, this is Abe Shannon, our new baseball coach." That introduction jolted me. It revealed what he had done to achieve his goal—used me to get Harry to give up baseball. It was all so clear. After Harry learned that Coach Rupp was indeed serious about wanting him to quit baseball and had hired me to take the No. 1 position, Harry quickly gave up coaching baseball and asked for his old job back. He got it too! Coach Rupp had taken him back, supposedly as his No. 2 assistant. I wondered how this arrangement would play out. I never mentioned anything about this to Coach Rupp or to Harry. My contract stated what my job was, and basketball practice did not start until October 15. I would wait and see what happened next. I stayed busy in my office working on the recruiting program, which I was surprised to learn had not been organized, and I also redesigned the conditioning program I had used at Regis.

In early August, I asked Coach Rupp for his permission to start a strengthening and conditioning program the day classes started. He balked at first, saying he had never done anything like that before, but I convinced him of the value of starting the players six weeks prior to practice with running and weightlifting exercises. I explained doing so would eliminate blisters, shin splints, pulled muscles, and fatigue. I told him, "It will build their stamina, which is the very thing they need. By the time you are ready to start practice in October, your players will be ready."

Then I reminded him of his custom of limiting his first week of practice to only one hour, so that the players could gradually get used to working. I promised him he would not have to do that anymore if he would let me have them for six weeks. He said, "Well, all right. Sounds good. Go ahead with it."

Because of NCAA regulations, we could not offer athletes any special treatment. We had to advertise all over campus that we were starting a conditioning and strengthening program and that anyone who wanted to participate could sign on. I don't recall anyone doing so.

When school started, the returning players were shocked to learn they were in a conditioning program. Some were out of shape from the summer. A few who had been there the previous year griped about what I was asking them to do. The freshmen did not seem to mind.

September can be pretty hot and humid in Kentucky, and exercising on those hot days outside was not pleasant. Three days each week we ran sprints and lifted weights. The other two days we ran cross-country distances. I began by letting players run 220-yard dashes. I had them run the track, walk back, run again. I clocked what they did. At the end of the program, the players could successfully run fifteen at forced intervals. I wanted them all to do the runs in less than thirty-two seconds. If it took a boy longer than that, he had to practice more. At first running did make some of them sick. I remember that Larry Conley threw up on the walk back every day that first week. After he took my advice to eat much earlier in the day and give his food plenty of time to digest, he did much better.

After a couple of days, two of the returning players went to Coach Rupp, saying that they represented the entire group and they all felt my program was torture, that it was "killing" them, and that a few guys were ready to quit. They wanted him to tell me to let up some on the running. When Coach Rupp came to me with their complaints, I invited him to come watch us.

The next day, he and I sat on the finish line to observe, and some of the boys put on a show for him but one especially did an outstanding performance. About the fifth two hundred, Pat Riley collapsed in front of us, pretending he was having a seizure. He twitched, sobbed, and drooled as he lay facedown in the dust. We watched as the dust traveled back up the spittle into his mouth. Concerned, Coach Rupp looked at me and asked, "Joe, what are you going to do?" I said, "Coach, I am going to give him an Academy Award for his acting and put him back on the track." Hearing that, Riley got up, staggered back across the field, and completed his running.

Next day, I gave Pat permission to miss practice because he had to take an accounting test. When another boy, Louie Dampier, said he, too, needed to take that test, I informed him, much to his surprise, that he was not enrolled in the accounting class.

Unlike the others, Louie Dampier did not try to hide his disdain for the program, and although he would do well on the short runs, he made little effort on the half mile and mile runs. That annoyed me. One day after we had finished the laps and were going into the weight room, I told him, "Louie, if I were coach, I would kick you off the team. You act like some kind of prima donna." As it turned out, it was fortunate that I was not the coach and that Louie was on the team. He turned out to be one of our very best players, one of our highest scorers. As for his dislike of my conditioning program, I learned years later that because his legs were shorter than the other players', running long stretches was just not something he could do easily.

Another time, after we had started formal practice, I called Louie a diva because his defense was so lacking. I told him he could not have played for me at Regis because of his poor defense. My criticism seemed to have a good effect on him, though. On December 18, 1965, we were in the finals of the University of Kentucky Invitational Tournament (UKIT). We were playing Indiana, which had a fast and high-scoring guard. Louie was assigned to guard him, and he really came forward with an outstanding performance in stopping that Indiana star guard. Toward the end of the game, I complimented him on his great defense. He smiled and asked, "Coach, could I play for you at Regis now?"

That first year, some of the boys worried that weightlifting would mess up their ability to shoot. So I encouraged them go to the gym directly after weightlifting to shoot for a while to maintain their shooting skills.

When Coach Rupp held his first practice on October 15, he and Harry were delighted to find the varsity in great shape and ready to work. They let me know how pleased they were, and from that day on my conditioning program has been a permanent part of the entire program. Now nearly all colleges, I suppose, have similar programs.

Many of the players who were in that first program have since written and talked about how much it helped them. They said they appreciated the results they got from it, and they gave the program credit for their success. Thad Jarez, who was on the heavy side when he started, often said how much it helped him slim down and made him a much better player. Larry Conley, along with others, has talked and written about how much it helped him.

20

Adjusting to Coach Rupp's Routines

It is not the strongest of the species that survives, nor the most intelligent, but the one most responsive to change. You have to be willing to change.

Charles Darwin

On the afternoon of October 15, 1965, about fifteen minutes before our first practice was to start at 3:00, I was in my office working when Coach Rupp, dressed for practice in his khakis, stuck his head in the door and asked, "What are you doing, Joe?" I told him I was working on the recruiting letters. He said, "Well, just go ahead and work on that. You can skip practice. *Harry* and I will take care of it." He closed the door and left. Stunned, I asked myself, "What did he just say? Did he not hire me as his No. 1 assistant?" I took a couple of deep breaths and wondered what he had done now.

I have never felt I needed a job so badly that I would keep it under any conditions. I always knew that I could make a living doing many other things. That afternoon, when my job did not appear to be what my contract said it was, I was ready to resign. I walked into the athletic director's office and asked Bernie, "What did Coach Rupp hire me as?" Bernie looked up at me, puzzled, and answered, "First assistant basketball coach. Why?" I replied, "I want to know if I am right before I resign." Then I told him what Coach Rupp had said to me. Bernie stood up and said, "Well, I be damned. You go get dressed and go to practice. I'll see about this." And that was all that was ever said about the matter.

You may be wondering now why I did not resign. I stayed for

several reasons. First of all, I did not want to uproot my family again; they had already moved so many times for me. Katharine and the children were happy living in Lexington near family and friends. By then, too, I had made friends and had earned the respect of many people I admired. A second reason was I could understand why Coach Rupp wanted Harry as his first assistant. Harry had been with him for nearly twenty years by then, and although they occasionally fussed and cussed each other, on the floor they worked together perfectly. What I could not understand was why Coach Rupp felt he had to use me to accomplish his goal of getting Harry to give up coaching baseball, for it was obvious that he had planned all along for me to be his recruiter.

Another reason I stayed is I love Kentucky. I love the University of Kentucky Wildcats. I had a passionate desire to contribute to its great tradition. I love coaching. I love the smell of that gym, the silence and seriousness of practices—no sounds except that of a basketball slapping the floor and boys running up and down the court. I love the tension and excitement of the games and helping young men achieve success that they did not even know they were capable of achieving. Coaching the Wildcats is what God created me to do.

After that day, I continued to work hard on the recruiting and the schedule, which Coach Rupp had only begun. The older he got, the less interest he had in doing any recruiting outside the city limits. The way he figured, boys ought to be coming to him begging to be on his team. He left recruiting to Harry and me. I went to practice every day I was in town. No one ever interfered with anything I did. No one, not Coach Rupp, Bernie Shively, or Harry, ever questioned me about my hours or anything else. They were all pleased with my work. I was left pretty much to myself to make my own travel schedule, and I liked it that way.

The job of recruiting is not easy when you are married with children. I did my best not to be away from my family any more often than I had to be. I always tried to get home as early in the evenings as possible, although I frequently did not succeed as well as I hoped. That always bothered me.

Things went along smoothly until the day Coach Rupp zapped me with another surprise. Minutes before our first game in November 1965, I discovered something that set me on fire—he had left no place on the front bench for me to sit. He had me sitting with the team managers. I went straight to him and asked, "What do you mean not leaving a place for me on the front bench? How do you think that makes me look to the players and to the boys I am recruiting? I'll tell you how it looks! It belittles me; it is demeaning me in their eyes and in the eyes of the public. You will not diminish my authority in that way." He knew I was angry. Without a word, he quickly made a place for me next to Harry, who sat next to him, and that's where I sat until Harry became athletic director.

Coach Rupp and I got along fairly well after that episode. I guess I was as close to him as anyone else in the program except Harry. But Harry never socialized with him. Coach Rupp's real friends, so to speak, were his banker, his doctor, his lawyer, his farm manager, and his pharmacist—professionals he needed quick access to. My wife and I were never invited to his home for dinner or for any other social reason. However, he'd ask me to go to lunch with him two or three times a week, and I'd go. He loved soups and chili; he thought steaks, which I enjoyed, were overrated. According to him, Brookings made the best chili, so we went there often. But we went to other good places too, like the Wildcat Lounge, Springs Motel Dining Room, and Cliff Hagan's Steak House, which was way out on the edge of town in those days. Neither Bernie nor Harry ever went with us, or with him when I couldn't go.

Whenever and wherever it was just the two of us alone and away from the campus, we always had a good time. He was relaxed and a different person. Some of our best times occurred when I drove him to make his speeches. He was a great public speaker and was frequently invited to speak to Rotaries, Lions Clubs, civic clubs, and organizations of all kinds. Also, he did many basketball clinics. We traveled a good bit in those days. We went to places all over Kentucky and out of it, too. In conversing on those drives, he was always pleasant and amusing. He loved telling funny stories, and he told them well. He kept a stockpile of them written out on index cards in a filing cabinet in his office. I heard most of them more than once through the years. But that was okay. We laughed a lot together then. I believed he liked and respected me, but I knew that he had to be in control at all times. He was a complex man, with different personalities in different situations.

As we drove through small towns on mostly two-lane roads, he was always interested in how many cars were parked in front of motels, restaurants, and other businesses, and how many television antennae were on houses. He had a keen interest in business affairs and how things were going in the small towns. He liked to see farms, plowed grounds, crops in the fields, or cattle munching in the meadows. He was a huge fan of farmers and cattlemen and liked to talk to them. In 1941 he bought a two-hundred-acre farm where he raised Hereford cattle. He was president of the Hereford Association for sixteen consecutive years. Wherever we stopped to get gas or a cold drink, he was most cordial to everyone we met. He would shake hands and speak with every person present as if he were running for an elected office. He was a big celebrity then, you know, and many people were thrilled to shake his hand.

When we would get close to where we were going, he would tell me, "Now, Joe, pull over and park here." The first time he told me to do that, I said, "But Coach, we are over a block away from where you are going to give your talk." He said, "That's okay. You never want to arrive early! You always want to be a little late and have your hosts standing outside the building searching around for you. You see, you want them to worry that you are not going to make it. That way they are so appreciative when they see you even though you are five or ten minutes late." So that's what we always did every time—arrive early and sit in the car until we were a few minutes late, and then pull up in front our destination, where a parking space had been provided for us.

Sure enough, there would be the hosts standing on the sidewalk anxiously looking around and then breaking into big smiles when they saw us pull up. He would give his talk, which everyone would thoroughly enjoy. Audiences always thanked him profusely. Everyone who ever heard him talk will agree he was an outstanding speaker—knowledgeable, informative, entertaining, amusing, and charming. No question about that!

On our drive back to Lexington, he would, with almost childlike glee, look forward to telling Jane Rawlings, his secretary, and Harry what a great success he had been. With his usual hyperbole, he'd say to them, "Oh, you should have seen how they packed the room! There was such a huge crowd, people lined the walls. Not enough chairs for everyone to sit. They loved me, too! And it was all adults—no children." Most of what he told them was true.

One year we got an invitation from the armed forces to come to Alaska—to Anchorage and Fairbanks—to conduct basketball clinics for the armed services. Now that was fun! The army treated us royally. We traveled as brigadier generals and were treated as such! We had a wonderful time on that trip.

We dressed in army attire and dined with the officers until we discovered that the food served to the enlisted men was so much better and heartier. We ate in the mess hall with them after that. One afternoon while we were in our room on the second floor of our accommodations, I had my chair tilted back leaning against the wall, and Coach Rupp was lying propped up in the bed. All of a sudden there was a loud noise and the floor under my feet buckled up. It was an earthquake! We learned later that a man in the room next to ours got so frightened he jumped out his second-story window. Fortunately, he was not seriously injured, and the earthquake lasted only a couple of minutes and did little damage.

The summer of 1966, Coach Rupp, Bernie, and Harry took the team to Tel Aviv, Israel, to play in the International Universities

Tournament. I stayed home to start a summer basketball training and conditioning camp for boys eight to fourteen years old. I had asked Coach Rupp if he wanted to join me in this project, but he said no.

Some of my friends who were coaches at other colleges accepted my offer, and we had our teams play in tournaments. My boys won trips to various places to compete and often won awards for their special skills. The camp was a great success, and I ran it for six years. It was a rewarding experience for all of us who were involved.

Before Coach Rupp left on the Tel Aviv trip, he told me he had been asked to write a book about training youths to play basketball. He asked me if I would write the book while he was gone, adding that it would, of course, bear his name only. He told me if I wrote the book while he was gone, he would split the $2,000 advance the publisher gave him and also split royalties with me. I wrote the book, and only his name was on the cover. It sold well. Time passed without his mentioning anything to me about the book. When I finally asked about my share of the royalties, he told me that it was his name that sold the book, and he had already paid me all I was to get.

21

More Adjusting to Coach Rupp's Routines

I have always envied the kind of coach who could go completely out of his mind and nobody would know the difference.

—Coach Adolph Rupp

I do not know what Coach Rupp was thinking when he said those words in the epigraph above. But I do know that he often did some things that gave me pause. Much of what he said was hilarious—whether he intended it to be funny or not. We all had trouble at times keeping a straight face while he was reprimanding some kid or even one of us. The way he created sarcastic punch lines was comedic, as were the expressions on his face. When it was just the two of us, he talked like a normal person, but sometimes when it was more than just us I never knew what to expect. I will give you a few examples.

One morning while he and I were in his office talking about where we were going for lunch, Mrs. Rawlings, his secretary, who sat at her desk in the little room outside his office, phoned him. He kept his speakerphone on, so I heard her say, "Coach Rupp, there is a reporter here who wants to talk to you." He shouted back, "Talk to me! I can't waste my time talking to him! You tell him I am too busy. Who the hell is it anyway?" She said, "It is Billy Reed. He says he only needs five minutes with you." "Billy Reed, dammit! That little —— better not take longer than five minutes."

Well, Billy Reed could hear every word he said and looked pale when he walked in. "Coach Rupp, sir," he said, "I just want to ask you about that kid you want to recruit from the Catholic high school." "Well, what do you want know? Ask your question and get the hell out of here!" He answered the question and then went on to have a nice fifteen-minute or so chat with Billy.

Not long after he had hired me to be his assistant, Coach Rupp and his wife invited Katharine and me to go with them to Red Mile Trotting Track. The track that day was having a drawing for a mink coat, and the winner would be announced immediately after the race. Katharine said that although she had never been lucky enough to win anything, she still wanted her name in that box. Mrs. Rupp, who already had a mink coat, added her name too.

Toward the end of the race, Coach Rupp stood up and told us to get ready to go because he wanted to "beat the traffic." Being caught in traffic was something he could not stand. Our wives frowned and said they wanted to stay for the drawing. Katharine gave me a hard stare. I pleaded, "Coach Rupp, let's wait to hear the results of the drawing. They are getting ready to do it now. It will just take a few minutes. The ladies want to know who won the coat." He refused, saying, "They are not going to win! I want to leave now. Let's go!"

As we were in the parking lot, heading toward our car, we heard the voice over the loudspeaker announce, "Katharine Hall is the winner of the mink coat! Katharine Hall, come to the speaker's table, please!" Stunned, we all stopped in our tracks. I told Katharine, "I will run back in." And run I did! But before I could get through the thick crowd and back up the steps to where the drawing was held, another name had been drawn.

That winter I had to buy Katharine a mink coat.

Early one dark, cold December morning, Harry, Coach Rupp, Dr. Jackson, the team's longtime physician, and I had to go to a game in Louisville. Standing in the hallway outside their offices, Coach Rupp and Harry started arguing over whose car to take.

Harry usually drove on those trips, but this time he said, "Let's take that new Oldsmobile the dealership has so generously provided for you." Coach Rupp didn't like that idea at all. Neither of them wanted to get their car dirty. Coach Rupp stated, "No! We will take your car and you drive!" Dr. Jackson and I went on and got into the backseat of Harry's big Cadillac while they continued to argue.

Harry was so angry that when we got on the highway, he rolled down all the windows. It was freezing! Coach Rupp yelled, "Harry, what the hell are you doing? Roll the —— windows up." Harry said, "No! I will not! This is *my* car." Dr. Jackson and I kept silent and scrunched down in our seats, turning our coat collars up around our faces and tying our scarves over our heads. It was a quiet, uncomfortable, and damp trip to Louisville.

When we arrived at Freedom Hall, where the game was to be played, rain was pouring down. Harry was good enough to let us out at the front door while he parked the car. Then, when we got ready to leave, it turned out that Harry had forgotten where he had parked it. We had to search the parking lot, which by then was flooded. Our pant legs got wet and our shoes filled with water as we wandered around for several minutes before I spotted Harry's car. The windows were rolled up on the way back but it was an unnecessarily miserable trip.

But even the misery of that event was overshadowed on another occasion. My friend Quack Butler (yes, that was what he was called) from Owensboro, Kentucky, came to my office one morning wanting to know if I would go to lunch with him and his boss. Quack sold encyclopedias for Compton's and was in town to meet with his sales manager. When I accepted his offer, he asked, "Do you reckon the old man will go with us?" I asked him, "Are you paying?" He answered, "Yes!" I said, "Then, sure, he'll go."

I walked across the hall to Coach Rupp's office and said, "Hey, Quack Butler is in town and wants to take us to lunch today. He's buying! Do you want to go?" Coach Rupp stood up and grabbed his hat, saying, "By all means! If we can get a free lunch off that tightwad, we'd better take it."

Quack, who could not help but hear him, was delighted. The poor guy did not know what he was in for. He had been happily thinking how impressed his boss would be that this very famous coach had accepted his invitation.

We all went outside to the car where the sales manager had been sitting behind the wheel waiting for us. Coach Rupp got in the front passenger seat, the way he always did, no matter whose automobile it was. Quack and I sat in the back. Introductions were made pleasantly, but what was about to unfold was not pleasant.

Neither of those men knew, much less suspected, that Coach Rupp was the worst of the worst of backseat drivers. Whenever we were in the car with other people, not just the two of us, he talked the entire time, giving the poor driver instructions and directions, cussing every red and yellow light, cussing any pedestrian walking across the street, and cussing the slow cars in front of ours.

He hated being stopped for red lights. He always told the driver to go on through red lights. When he saw the caution light come on, he would shout, "Don't stop! Keep going! Keep going! Quick, get through that yellow light. Noooo, don't let that old woman start to cross on that yellow! Hurry! Keep going!"

If we got to a railroad crossing too late and had to wait for a train to pass, he'd cuss every train car that rolled passed us. He sometimes behaved this way even when Mrs. Rupp was with us. But after listening to him for only a few minutes, she'd put a stop to it. She'd say firmly, "Adolph, now that's enough." And he would quit, though we could tell it was painful for him to do so.

I was hoping he would settle down after we were in the restaurant, but he didn't. He complained about everything—the waitress was too slow, his soup was too cold, his iced tea was too warm. The moment we sat down, he surprised us by saying that he absolutely had to be back in his office by 1:00 and we needed to leave in plenty of time for him to get back. We all needed to hurry. He could not be late for his appointment.

As we headed back to the campus, his directions for the "shortest" route unfortunately took us over train tracks. As fate would have it, we heard the train whistle just before we reached the tracks. While the train was passing, we had to listen to him rage about how incompetent the city planners and the railroad companies were to have trains pass right through the center of big cities, delaying the flow of traffic.

I can only imagine what the poor sales manager and Quack thought, but both surely had to be surprised and disappointed. Then, when we reached the campus and got out of the car, Coach Rupp's demeanor changed entirely. He shook the driver's hand and said most graciously what a pleasure it had been to meet him. He shook hands with Quack and thanked him for taking us to lunch.

He and I walked to our offices. I watched him pick up a newspaper from his secretary's desk, go into his office, prop his feet up on his desk, and start reading. He did not have a 1:00 appointment.

While I was a student at UK years earlier and one of the subs on Coach Rupp's bench, I learned about some of his superstitions. Much later, as his assistant, I discovered just how seriously superstitious he was.

On game day at home, he would always eat with the players at 4:00 in the afternoon in the Student Union. They would have a light meal of a small piece of steak, a baked potato, and a piece of toast—something that wouldn't disturb their stomachs. The trainers at one point got the idea that we should have a pasta meal, so we went to that for a while. But the players didn't like it, so we went back to a small steak menu.

After eating, Coach Rupp would have the boys go back to their rooms and rest. He wanted them to get off their feet and lie down. They were not to go shopping or even go downtown. They were not to play pool. He wanted them to stay off their feet. They were to go straight to their rooms, lie down on their beds, and rest until the time came to go to the Coliseum for the game warm-up.

He had a pre-game ritual that he scrupulously followed. After the meal, he would leave the Student Union and walk (exactly the same way every time) the short distance to Memorial Coliseum, which was where our offices were and where our games were played. When he came to the manhole cover on the sidewalk near the side entrance to the Coliseum, he stepped on it—with his right foot only—before he entered the building.

After entering the Coliseum, he'd go into the locker room, where the managers always kept a Kleenex box in the third locker (I think) on the right. He took one tissue from the Kleenex box unless a manager was there to hand him one. He always took just one Kleenex. After he cleaned his eyeglasses with the tissue, he would wad it up and throw it on the *floor* next to the wastebasket. One of the managers would spread out in his hand three sticks of chewing gum—Juicy Fruit, Beechnut, and Spearmint (I think that was the order they were supposed to be in)—and offer them to Coach Rupp, who always chose the one in the middle. Then he rolled up the paper wrapper and threw it on the floor beside the trash can. Never in it! Someone else would have to pick up his trash. Also, he also carried his lucky buckeye in his brown suit coat pocket. And whenever he played a Catholic school, he always invited a Catholic priest to sit somewhere near him.

He would take a copy of the program, mark the starters, roll the program up, and stick it in my coat pocket. I would take it to the scorer's table and show it to the scorers so they would know who our starters were for that night's game. I got into the habit of keeping the rolled-up program in my hand and using it for a pointer. After I got to be head coach, I was so used to holding a rolled-up program that I used it as a pre-game ritual. That hand-held rolled-up program became part of my persona.

Coach Rupp's greatest superstition involved finding pennies

or hairpins before a game. Whenever he walked, he would look for both of those things. He'd often find them in the parking lots or on the streets. If he found a penny with the head facing up, he was extremely happy, and his attitude was positive. If he found a hairpin, he believed that was a sure sign of victory. If the open end of the hairpin was pointing toward him, that meant he was going to win by a big score.

After he developed an ulcerated foot condition and couldn't go on longer walks, it became the job of the managers to plant hairpins on his route to the bus or in front of his hotel room. And sometimes when they were in a hurry, they would just dump the whole box outside his room. He would be so happy. He'd say, "By George, look what I found, Joe!" He would stoop down and pick up a handful of hairpins and put them in his pocket along with his buckeye, grinning as if he had just won a championship. Coach Rupp didn't seem to know that his managers were scattering those items for him to find, or if he did, it didn't seem to matter.

I have never known anyone else who was as superstitious as Coach Rupp. He lost a game one time when he was wearing a blue suit, and he never wore blue to games after that. He would always wear a brown suit, a brown felt hat, and brown shoes and socks.

One time when the African American porter who took coats near the entrance to the stadium was absent, home ill, Coach Rupp got very upset because he always shook hands with that porter before every home game. Shaking that man's hand was a significant part of his ritual. He had to shake that man's hand. He sent a manager to the porter's home to bring him to the stadium just so he could shake his hand and then be driven home.

My parents, Bill and Ruth Hall, with my sister Laura Jane.

My dad, Charles "Bill" C. Hall, 1980.

My birthplace in Cynthiana, Kentucky.

My childhood home in Cynthiana.

Me, about four years old, on my first vehicle.

My fifth-grade school photo.

Me, my sister, and our dog, Herman.

Cynthiana's football team during my junior year in high school. I'm number 50, fourth from the left in the front row. Coach Bill Boswell stands at the top left.

Cynthiana High School; I graduated in 1947.

Friends (*left to right*): Myron Hill, me (holding Kenton Barnett, Jimmy Lee Barnett's brother), John Swinford, Lane Taylor (kneeling), Jimmy Lee Barnett.

Me and Laura Jane Hall.

Heading to the pool in my Model-T Ford, which I painted in my school colors, green and white. *Left to right:* me, Lane Taylor, Moose Florence.

Walking to school one mile in the snow, 1946.

Working in a tobacco field on Uncle Harney's farm in Bourbon County.

My high school photo,
senior year, 1947.

I am number 3 on the East-West High School All-Star Team coached
by Earle Jones. His Maysville, Kentucky, team won the state tournament
that year—1947. This is the summer Coach Rupp gave me a basketball
scholarship.

UK's 1948–1949 basketball team; I'm number 31 in the front row.

Coach Varnell and the Sewanee team. I'm number 19.

On October 27, 1951, six weeks after our first date, I married Katharine Dennis.

Katharine and me with our children and their spouses (*standing left to right*): Rick and Judy Derrickson, Steve Hall, Kathy Hall Summers, and Mike Summers.

My first job: coaching basketball and football at Shepherdsville High School in Shepherdsville, Kentucky.

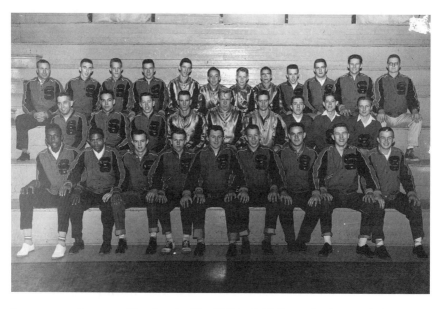

In my second year at Shepherdsville, 1956–1957, I coached "S" Club football, basketball, and baseball.

After Shepherdsville, I (*second from left*) moved to Regis College in Denver, Colorado, where I was first assistant coach and later head coach.

Regis wins the Nebraska Wesleyan Invitational Tournament.

A friendly handwritten note from Coach Adolph Rupp.

The 1964 Olympic Trials Team.

(*Right*) In 1965 Coach
Rupp hired me as
assistant coach and
recruiter for the 1965–
1966 season.

(*Below*) Coach Rupp
with first assistant coach
Harry Lancaster and me.

Coach Rupp never sat on the bench after I became head coach. This photo was taken after Harry resigned and I became Coach Rupp's first assistant.

After Coach Rupp retired, I became head coach in 1972.

Me and assistants Ray Edelman, Lynn Nance, Dick Parsons, and Leonard Hamilton. (University of Kentucky general photographic prints)

Sophomores Joey Holland, Larry Johnson, Ernie Whitus, and Merion Haskins. (University of Kentucky general photographic prints)

Seniors who played in the NCAA championship game in 1975: Jimmy Dan Conner, Kevin Grevey, Bob Guyette, Jerry Hale, G. J. Smith, and Mike Flynn. (University of Kentucky general photographic prints)

Freshmen and 1978 NCAA champs Rick Robey, Dan Hall, James Lee, Jack Givens, and Mike Phillips. (University of Kentucky general photographic prints)

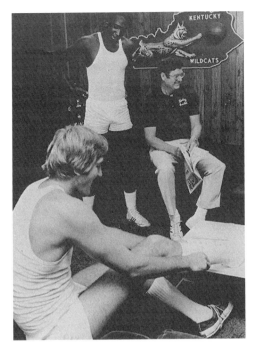

In the training room lounge: Bob Guyette (*foreground*), Jack Givens, and me. (University of Kentucky general photographic prints)

Supervising the running program. (University of Kentucky general photographic prints)

On the farm. (University of Kentucky general photographic prints)

Here I am in a familiar
sideline stance, program
in hand. (Portrait Print
Collection, University
of Kentucky)

Tension during the 1978 championship game with Duke.

The 1978 NCAA championship.

My first-season win against Tennessee at the SEC championship game, 1973.

USA NATIONAL MEN'S BASKETBALL TEAM
WORLD INVITATIONAL TOURNAMENT "CONVERSE CUP" CHAMPIONS
April 5-9, 1978

1. USA   2. Yugoslavia   3. USSR   4. Cuba

Sitting (l-r): Joe B. Hall, Head Coach (Kentucky); Jack Givens (Kentucky); Sidney Moncrief (Arkansas); Jay Shidler (Kentucky); Kyle Macy (Kentucky); James Lee (Kentucky); Mike O'Koren (North Carolina); Dick Parsons, Assistant Coach (Kentucky).
Standing (l-r): Keith Webster, Trainer (Kentucky); Jim Bailey (Rutgers); David Greenwood (UCLA); Joe Barry Carroll (Purdue); Rick Robey (Kentucky); Larry Bird (Indiana State); Earvin Johnson (Michigan State); Bill Keightly, Manager (Kentucky).
Insets (absent for team photo): Left - Phil Ford (North Carolina); Right - Darrell Griffith (Louisville).

The first USA National Men's Basketball Invitational Tournament, 1978.

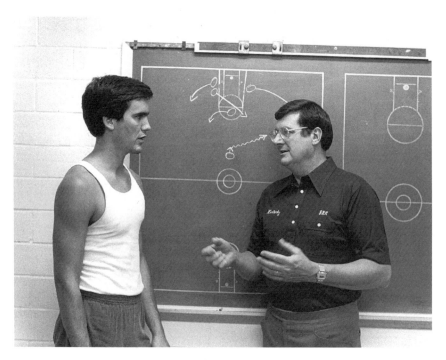

Me with Kyle Macy.

Japanese National team visits Lexington for workouts under me and my assistants.

Japanese women's pro team of the Sekisui Chemical Company in Kyoto.

Rupp Arena under construction.

Joe B. Hall Wildcat Lodge. (*Lexington Herald-Leader*)

My statue on UK's campus. (UPK photo)

Me with former governors Bert Combs and Ned Breathitt, fishing in Ash Rapids Camp in Canada.

(*Left*) Goose hunting with Governor Julian Carroll. (*Right*) Trophy crappie at Kentucky Lake.

(*Left*) Giving Tubby Smith putting tips. (*Right*) Me with Arnold Palmer.

Sharing popcorn with
Governor Martha
Layne Collins.

Katharine and me with President Jimmy Carter and wife, Rosalynn.

The Joe B. and Denny Show.

Doing color commentary
for ABCTV.

Beloved Wildcat equipment manager Bill Keightley.

Stealing Denny's popcorn.

"The Big Three": Crum, Calipari, and me.

In retirement: after the crowd spells "K-E-N-T-U-C-K," I make the "Y."

Me with Marianne Walker.

22

Recruiting

I give Coach Hall a lot of credit for enabling our team to reach the NCAA National Championship in 1966, because he brought in a conditioning program and a new look to the program. It was something Coach Rupp needed at that point in time.

Larry Conley

While I was at Regis, I had to work with a very small recruiting budget. Oftentimes I had to use my own money for expenses. At UK the situation was far different: the recruiting program was well financed, and I had money to travel wherever I needed to go to scout, as often as I needed. I could take players and their parents to some good restaurants for dinner. I could have them fly to UK for a campus tour and to meet Coach Rupp and Coach Lancaster. For the first time in my coaching career, I could really do some serious recruiting. I wanted intelligent young men with good character who had a passion for basketball. It helped immensely if they understood what it means to be a member of a team. And I found many such young men, too.

Although my budget was generous, the recruiting program had never been organized, so I set about designing a system much like the one I had at Regis. My system was actually based on the training that I had gotten working as a salesman for the Heinz Company years earlier. I had an excellent sales manager who told me that not only did I have to sell to existing customers, but I also had to find new ones, and he taught me how to do that. In selling anything, he said, it is usually the seventh contact that seals the deal. I, too, came to believe there is something special about seven contacts.

In setting up the program at UK, I formulated seven steps, more or less. After I had identified players who interested me, I wrote each one a handwritten letter because I had no secretary to type for me. I learned later that my handwritten letters made a great first impression. The recipients, and especially their parents, appreciated them. They said they conveyed a friendlier introduction than the typed form-like ones they had gotten from other institutions. Through the years, many have told me they still have their letters.

In that first letter, I would include a self-addressed postcard asking general information about their success as a player and their college interest. When I received that card back, I knew the sender was interested in talking to me. Then I would reply, asking him to send me his grade transcript and his complete schedule. I would follow up by sending him information about our program and school. In other words, I kept a correspondence going between us because each of my letters required a response. After I received the last response, I would visit his home, meet with him and his parents, and take them all out to dinner.

Although my budget permitted me to do those things, I always used it wisely as I am by nature a frugal person. However, that didn't stop Coach Rupp from complaining. "Joe, you are spending far too much feeding these people." He always had a strong objection to what he considered high food bills. He could not tolerate them, but he did not like to see other kinds of charges either, no matter how insignificant. He was, as old-timers used to say, as tight as the bark on a tree.

For example, Baldy Gibbs, one of the guys who scouted our opponents, would travel with us. Every morning, he would buy a newspaper, which cost maybe 10 or 20 cents. When he reported his travel expenses, he would include the cost of the newspapers. Coach Rupp chewed him out one day, asking, "Don't you get the newspaper at home?" Baldy replied, "Yes, but I am not home, and I like to read a newspaper every day." Coach Rupp brought the subject up again and again, but Baldy didn't pay any attention to him.

Coach Rupp didn't like to see the boys charging for what he considered extras, such as pricey desserts. Whenever we traveled for games, he saw to it that the boys ordered what he considered "sensibly priced" meals and "no fancy desserts, just ice cream." Three or four scoops of ice cream were sufficient. Every afternoon, the athletic director's office would give him a record of what each player on scholarship had charged for food. If he thought a boy was charging too much for his meals, he would jump on him, call him into his office, and ask him if he had invited guests to dine with him. "*Nobody*," he would yell, "can consume this much food at one meal!" The plain fact was all the players were big, tall young men who were very active and had hearty appetites. They could and did consume a lot of food at each meal.

Only a few of my recruiting meal expenses were unusually high, like the time I had a recruit order escargot, not even knowing what it was but because it was the most expensive item on the menu. I will never forget the look of horror on the boy's face when the waiter placed a little plate of snails in front of him. His father, sitting across from him watching, said sternly, "You ordered them! You eat them!"

Once I went to Dayton, Ohio, where I visited with a coach and his wife about one of his players. The coach was good enough to pick me up at the airport so I would not have to rent a car. I asked him to take us to a nice restaurant for dinner, at my expense, so we could discuss the purpose of my visit. We had cocktails before our meals of prime rib, twice-baked potato, and Caesar salad. Our dessert of crème brûlée was delicious, but expensive.

Sure enough, the next day, Coach Rupp questioned me about my expenses for that trip. I pointed out that even though my meal expenses were higher than usual, I had saved money by not having to rent a car.

A few days later, as I was preparing to leave again, he said he was going with me. I said, "That will be great, Coach Rupp. Then you can show me how to control the meal expenses. You take control of ordering the dinners this evening."

That afternoon Coach Rupp and I arrived at the prospect's house and were greeted by the recruit, his brother, and their parents. The recruit, his father, and his brother were all six foot seven or six foot eight. Each one weighed well over two hundred pounds. We had a very brief visit with his parents because they had an appointment elsewhere. The recruit asked if it would be all right if his brother went to dinner with us. Coach Rupp said, "Certainly."

We took them to the nicest restaurant in town. Coach Rupp quickly scanned the menu, saw that spaghetti and meatballs was the least expensive dish, and said, "Hummm! That spaghetti and meatballs sounds awfully good. Don't you all think so? That's what I will have." He thought the boys would follow his lead and order the same, but instead they ignored his suggestion. The boy asked his older brother what he wanted for dinner. The brother answered, "I can't decide between the prime rib and the rainbow trout." The waiter said to him, "Well, you're a big boy. Why don't you order both?" And he did! I wish I could describe the look on Coach Rupp's face then. The recruit ordered the largest prime rib steak and all the sides that were available. They both had fabulous desserts.

I had the devil of a time trying not laugh as I looked at Coach Rupp. His lips were clamped down tightly and turned downward in his disapproval frown. He wouldn't even look at me. He stared at the boys as they happily began to chow down. After we took them home and started back to Lexington, I could not restrain myself any longer and broke down laughing so hard that I had to take my glasses off. I just could not keep from saying, "Coach, you taught me a lot tonight!" His response was one I will not repeat.

As a result of Coach Rupp's complaints about my expenses, Bernie Shively, the athletic director, visited my office one day and told me he knew how important recruiting was to the success of our program, and he was giving me a personal recruiting budget that I did not have to clear through Coach Rupp. He said, "In fact, he will never see your account anymore." After that I never heard another word about my budget from Coach Rupp.

Gradually my recruiting program grew more sophisticated and successful, appropriate for a large university such as ours. These young athletes I was interested in were being pursued by other coaches as well, or for one reason or another were seriously considering signing with another school. I had to be persistent. By the time many of them signed the UK contract, I would have made just about seven contacts with them. Of course, some recruits knew right away they wanted to come to Kentucky and signed quickly. For some of the others, it took persuasion. I recruited some great athletes too. Men such as Tom Parker, Larry Steele, Dan Issel, Mike Pratt, Larry Stamper, Jim Andrews, Jerry Hale, Terry Mills, Jim Dinwiddie, Dwane Casey, Stan Key, Kevin Grevey, and so many others of that high caliber.

My time at UK coincided with a controversial and turbulent period not only in college basketball but in the nation itself. Early in the 1960s, Governor Ned Breathitt and Dr. John W. Oswald, president of the university from 1963 to 1968, wanted to integrate all UK's athletic teams. Before I came to Kentucky in 1965, Coach Rupp had been unsuccessful in his attempts to recruit any African American athletes. On more than one occasion, he and Harry had visited Westley Unseld, one of the top five high school recruits in 1964, and his family at their home in Louisville. But Unseld decided to stay in his hometown and signed with the Cardinals at the University of Louisville. Also in 1965, Butch Beard from Hardinsburg said he really liked UK, but he too signed with the Cardinals, no doubt because his friends were there. Nearly everyone in Hazard, Kentucky, urged their hometown star Jimmy Rose to go to UK. Coach Rupp thought for sure he was going to sign him, but he chose Western in Bowling Green instead.

I believe Coach Rupp's early attempts to recruit black players failed primarily because reporters, broadcasters, and others stated that he was racist. And that's pretty much how he has gone down in history—as a racist. I was his assistant from 1965 to 1972—during that troubling integration period. He and I were in daily contact or communication. We took trips together: to games, clinics, visits to recruits, and his speaking engagements. Sometimes, during breaks in our hectic schedules, we would leave town and go fishing together. Even after he retired in 1972 and I became head coach, he continued to come to his office and stayed involved in the program. During all those years I was with him, of course, I often heard him be intolerant of some people, but I never once heard him be intolerant of anyone based *only* on that person's color, ethnicity, or religion. Coach Rupp had a hate list, it's true—and at the top of it was losing basketball games. He wanted men who would help him win games. Remember, he had been the winningest coach in the nation for decades, and he was determined to maintain that record.

In March 1966, our opponent in the NCAA championship game was Texas Western. Winning that game would have given Coach Rupp his *fifth* NCAA championship, which he desperately wanted—all of us did. I was there then, sitting on the bench with Coach Rupp. I saw it all. I heard it all. I know what happened. Going into that game, we had serious concerns. Two of our starters were not well: Pat Riley had a swollen, infected toe, and Larry Conley had the flu. He was sick while he played in the semi-finals against Duke. We nursed him the best we could, hoping he'd recover before the final game, but there was not enough time between the games for him to get well. Coach Rupp, with his faith in old-timey remedies, wanted us to find some goose grease to rub on Larry's chest; we gave him penicillin shots instead. I am not telling you this to make excuses for losing that game. I am telling you facts.

It is also a fact the Miners won that night because they played much better than we did. And we told them so. After the game, Pat Riley limped into the Miners' locker room and congratulated his fellow athletes. Showing great sportsmanship, Pat has often pointed out since then that the *right* team won that championship, and I heartily agree with him. The Miners' victory carved the way for integration and created much needed changes and opportunities for many young people.

Immediately after the game, the media began reporting that No. 1 Kentucky lost to the Miners because they did not know how to compete with black players, but the Cats had played against black players before, including the great Elgin Baylor of Seattle University. We won our fourth NCAA title in 1958, when Coach Rupp's starters—Vernon Hatton, Johnny Cox, John Crigler, Ed Beck, and Adrian Smith—defeated Seattle 84–72. After that victory, we went on to win over Temple University, also an integrated team. Indeed, by 1966, there were many great African American basketball players, such as Wilt Chamberlain, Oscar Robertson, and Bill Russell, and even back in 1948, Coach Rupp had served as assistant coach of an integrated team in the Olympic trials.

Years later, Hollywood made a film—*Glory Road*—about that 1966 Kentucky versus Texas Western game, focusing on the black-white issue. Hollywood's version of that event is not what I experienced.

It is important to point out that none of the other SEC coaches had African Americans on their rosters at the time Coach Rupp didn't. Nor did Duke, which we beat in the national semi-finals in order to play Texas Western. Duke is in the Atlantic Coast Conference. Yet Coach Rupp was the one who got blistered for it, no doubt because his mouthy, egotistical, arrogant manner, plus his astonishingly long string of successes, made him fodder for the media and an easy target.

I think his age, his dour appearance, and his manner of speaking contributed to his reputation in the press. Although he could still impress large audiences with his great prepared talks laced with amusing anecdotes, on a one-on-one basis he did not always make such a good impression. He had a tendency to avoid looking directly at the person with whom he was speaking, and he kept his chin tilted up in the air. His smile looked more like a smirk.

He would tell players what an honor it was to receive a UK athletic scholarship and to play on his team. Neither he nor Harry appeared to be friendly or solicitous with anyone. With his flat-top haircut, broad shoulders, and strong physique, Harry looked and acted more like a military drill sergeant than a benevolent uncle or protective older brother. Coach Rupp did not present the image of a caring father or kind grandfather. He did not generate those good feelings.

Concerned parents, especially African American ones, needed to know that their sons were going to be looked after, protected by their coaches once they got to UK. But I don't think they got that feeling from talking with Coach Rupp and Harry. And they had no way of knowing that those two were never father figures to me or to any of the white players either.

When I arrived in 1965, I was much younger than Coach Rupp and Harry and had more energy and enthusiasm to recruit than they did. Also, I like people! I have always enjoyed meeting new people, and I try to approach them in a friendly manner. I have had good relationships with African Americans since I was a child, first playing and fishing with them while I was growing up; then, as a coach, I had black players on every team I ever coached. Coach Rupp and Dr. Oswald thought that I would surely succeed at integrating our team. I thought I would too, but I soon learned it was more difficult at first than I had imagined.

When I started my search to recruit, I used my friendships with the African American athletes on my previous teams as evidence that I was sincere. In fact, those players made introductory calls to recruits for me, but none of the ones we contacted wanted to come to Kentucky. I tried to convince my friend Cozel Walker from Clinton, Kentucky, to come play for us. He had one more year of college to be eligible to play. "Cozel," I told him, "if you come to Kentucky, you will be a great star. I know I could talk Coach Rupp into letting you sit a year to play." Cozel came to Regis with me, then followed me to Central Missouri when I moved there. I thought he would follow me to Kentucky, too, but he did not. He said he would go anywhere to be with me but, he explained, he would "not lead the crusade of integrating the South. I don't mind playing for Kentucky because I am from Kentucky, but I do not want to play in segregated places." And he had good reasons for feeling that way.

To learn what Cozel meant about not wanting "to lead the crusade," read about Perry Wallace, another player we tried to recruit. In 1966, Perry went to Vanderbilt, which thus became the first college in the Southeastern Conference to have an African American basketball player. And if you want to understand how difficult it was in those days for a pioneer black athlete to integrate into a white team, I urge you to read Andrew Maraniss's *Strong Inside: Perry Wallace and the Collision of Race and Sports in the South.* In this book, Perry recounts his experiences as a college student and a basketball player in his hometown of Nashville. He poignantly describes the meanness he endured; the loneliness and isolation he felt as a student and as a player; the fears he had of being shot on the court or on the street. He tells about the death threats that were sent to his family, and the petitions sent to his coach, Roy Skinner, to remove him. Perry had this to say about playing on the All-Star team for Coach Rupp: "He was extremely welcoming and gracious." The black UK players I know have always spoken kindly of Coach Rupp.

We at UK never had any trouble with death threats or shootings, as many other coaches had in some places. But while I was coaching at Regis, a spectator once threw a bottle at my African American player. It missed him and shattered on the wall. At that same game, while we were sitting on the bench, some people expressed their disdain and ignorance by throwing their cigarette butts at the player's feet.

Kentucky is the northernmost state in the Southeastern Conference, and so the bulk of our schedule required us to travel throughout the South. Black parents were wary of this for fear of how their sons would be treated—mistreated is the better word. In those days, in many places throughout the South, African Americans suffered many indignities. They could not eat in certain restaurants with white people, stay in many hotels or motels, or use public water fountains and restrooms. In movie houses, they had to sit only in a certain area, like the balcony. After I became head coach and we were on the road, I had to say to a restaurant owner on more than one occasion, "If you will not serve us all in your dining room, then serve all of us in the kitchen, please." I would not stop to buy gas at stations that would not let all of us use the restroom. I made reservations in hotels where I knew all of us could stay. Other than those things, I had no problems.

After I became head coach in 1972, I signed Reggie Warford, who turned out to be an outstanding athlete, coach, and citizen. He has been inducted into the High School Hall of Fame. Then I hired Leonard Hamilton, an African American, as my assistant, a wonderful guy. He stayed with me for ten years. I signed many other black basketball stars from Kentucky: Larry Johnson, Merion Haskins (named top alumnus by the agriculture department for his work teaching foreign countries how to raise tobacco), James Lee, Melvin Turpin, Dwane Casey, Paul Andrews, Charles Hurt, Freddie Cowan, Leroy Byrd, Winston Bennett, and Jack Givens, the first African American player from Kentucky to be named an All-American. He scored forty-one points, leading us to victory in a 1978 NCAA championship game against Duke.

Also, I added to my roster several other outstanding black basketball stars from out of state: LaVon Williams from Colorado, who was honored by the UK art department as one of the top artists in the nation; Kenny Walker and Cedric Jenkins from Georgia; Derrick Hord and Richard Madison from Tennessee; Dwight Anderson and Truman Claytor from Ohio; Sam Bowie and Clarence Tillman from Pennsylvania; James Blackmon from Indiana; and Ed Davender from New York.

I am proud of our athletes and the contributions they have made to our program and to the communities where they live. If I have left anyone's name out, forgive me. It was not done on purpose, and I apologize.

I thoroughly enjoyed recruiting because I like traveling and meeting new people. I had many memorable experiences recruiting too. For example, I knew I had to get Dan Issel. I had to! There was no doubt about it. I think I stayed in his town nearly a week trying to convince him to come to Kentucky. He had such great potential. He wanted to go to Wisconsin for personal reasons, but his parents thought Northwestern was better. Later, after visiting Kentucky with him, his dad leaned toward UK. The afternoon I arrived at his home in Batavia, Illinois, Dan wasn't there. His dad was outside painting. So I sat down on an upside-down bucket and talked to him. Dan came home and I had supper there with the family. Dan told me he had a date that night and could spend only an hour with me. I surprised him when I said, "That's all right. I'll wait till you return and talk with your parents." When his dad turned in at his regular bedtime—10:00 p.m.—I continued to stay and talk with his mom. Dan was surprised when he arrived home close to midnight and saw me still sitting in his living room. He was well worth waiting for. He is a seven-time All Star.

I found Jim Andrews, an outstanding player and person, by sheer luck. I was driving to Findlay, Ohio, to scout a player when I stopped in Lima at a service station to buy gas. In those days, service station employees, dressed in uniforms and caps, would pump the gas, check the air in your tires, clean your windshield, and tell you the local news. I always enjoyed talking with them. It was a nice service, and when the weather was bad, we didn't have to get out of the car. Those were the good old days!

That afternoon, I asked the young man if he knew of any good basketball players in his area. He said, "We sure do! We got a big guy, six foot ten or more, who averages about thirty-six points and twenty-two to twenty-three rebounds. He's playing tonight if you want to watch him." I followed his directions to the high school, watched that game, and was very impressed with the player—Jim

Andrews. I wanted to get him signed on that night, but he told me he had been approached by UCLA, Ohio State, and the University of Tennessee and was seriously considering signing with Coach Ray Mears there. We had a game coming up with UT, so I invited him to visit our campus and watch us play. He did, and after watching that game, he said he'd learned that he did not want to play UT's style of basketball. He much preferred the fast up-and-down style of the Wildcats. Jim was an outstanding athlete.

In all my experiences, I never had a recruit or his parents ask for special treatment or gifts, but I did have two high school coaches ask for travel money for the parents to come see their sons play. I said no and immediately stopped all contact with those coaches. In my talks with parents, recruits, and their coaches, I would always say recruits would not get cars or booster gifts, but they would get tuition, summer jobs, room, board, books, and fees.

I am proud of all our athletes and the contributions they have made to our program and to the communities where they live.

Now, after saying all of that about recruiting, I want to add that for anyone with a spouse and children, recruiting is not a good job. After we moved to Kentucky and I was given many recruiting responsibilities, I sometimes would not see my family for as long as a month or more. I would often get home late at night after the children had gone to sleep, and in the morning, they would have left for school before I awoke. It was not unusual on long trips for me to travel on private planes. After being away for a week, I would land in Lexington just long enough to meet Katharine at the airport for a short visit and to exchange my suitcase full of dirty clothes for the suitcase of clean ones and sundries that she had brought me. Those were difficult times for me, but especially hard for Katharine and the children.

23

Beginning of the End, 1967

On his death bed, I asked for a summation of his life. "Just say he did the best he could," Adolph said. "That's enough."

Russell Rice

On December 12, 1967, all of us were all shocked and saddened to learn that our friend Bernie Shively had died at his home suddenly of a heart attack. He was such a good man whom we all liked and respected.

One of the university vice presidents, Bob Johnson, was appointed acting athletic director while the search committee did its interviews for the position. After no one had been hired by 1968, a couple of the staff members, including Harry, made it known that they'd like to have the job. We were surprised by Harry's bid for the position because we all had assumed that he would be Coach Rupp's successor. He deserved the job of head coach, as loyal as he had been to Coach Rupp for years. We thought too that at this point Coach Rupp would announce that he recommended Harry to succeed him—but he never did. It did not matter because by then Harry had gotten tired waiting for him to step down and was ready to give up coaching entirely. Even if Coach Rupp finally did recommend him, Harry said, he didn't want the job—he was getting too old to deal with all the stress that went along with it.

When one of the administrators on the athletic board and on the board of trustees, Dr. Ralph Angelucci, called Harry to appoint him acting athletic director, I was not surprised, but Coach Rupp was! Harry gladly accepted, for he had always joked, even in front of Bernie, that "Shive" (as he called him) never worked hard; his job was so easy that he slept in his office most of the time.

The following year, 1969, the university made Harry the permanent athletic director, and in hardly any time at all, he was admitting how wrong he had been about how easy Shive's job was. Much to our amusement, Harry found that trying to please so many people, which is what the AD has to do, was far more difficult than he had imagined. We chuckled.

Coach Rupp was devastated without his "right-hand man" to assist him. He would go around saying, "What the hell does he want being an athletic director? What's he thinking?! Whoever heard the name of any athletic director! Nobody! Dammit!"

You see, the older Coach Rupp got, the more he had depended on Harry. Without him now, he was cranky. On September 2, 1969, when he turned sixty-eight, we all quietly went about our business, making no mention of it. Of course, the chatter outside our department now about his retirement and his replacement was getting much louder—and that made him angrier. By then, his appearance was that of an old, tired, and very sick but very stubborn man. He was behaving much like his own Kansas coach Phog Allen, who had to be physically carried, kicking and screaming, out of his office.

Yet when it was time for him to retire, Coach Rupp's loyal supporters beseeched President Singletary to waive the university's mandatory retirement age of seventy for him. They said that because he had had such a remarkable career, he should retire only when he was ready. I agreed with them!

Coach Rupp did indeed have a remarkable career. He was known as the "winningest coach in the nation." He had coached at UK from 1930 to 1972 and won 876 games—that's 82 percent of the games his teams played, more than any other coach at that time had won. It was not until 1977 that Dean Smith surpassed him. Coach Rupp's Wildcats won twenty-seven Southeastern Conference titles, one National Invitation Tournament (1946), and four National Collegiate Athletic Association championships (1948, 1949, 1951, 1958). Only one other coach—John Wooden—

had won more NCAAs than he at that time. I said then to anyone who would listen that Coach Rupp deserved to be allowed to retire only when he was ready to do so.

His anger worsened his physical problems, and he had to be hospitalized several times. Some wondered if he would even live to his seventieth birthday. Since his youth he had had back problems, which had been made worse by a botched surgery in the 1930s. After having a second back surgery, years later, to remove two discs, he continued to have back pain that slowed him down.

In addition, the poor man had high blood pressure, diabetes, vision problems, and at one time or another, lung congestion, swollen knees, and frightening trouble with his feet. He had a painful ongoing infection in one foot that doctors couldn't cure with any of the antibiotics available then. They were actually talking about removing his foot. Toward the end of his career, he often sat during games with his leg propped on a stool.

He took a handful of medications every day. He would get so tired in the afternoons that he sometimes fell asleep at his desk. Other times he didn't seem to be thinking clearly, but that may have been caused, we thought, by his seeing two different doctors and using prescriptions for high blood pressure medicines from both of them. After he and Dr. V. A. Jackson became close friends, Dr. Jackson straightened out his medications and saw to it that Coach Rupp took only what he prescribed. Also, Dr. Jackson traveled with us on our out-of-town games and always stayed in a room next to Coach Rupp's, ready to help him.

When Coach Rupp learned that Dr. Jackson had included the words "Physician for the Wildcats" on his name cards, he got angry. He said he had not appointed him the team's doctor. After I became head coach, I went ahead and named the deserving Dr. Jackson the official Wildcat physician.

By the time I had arrived in 1965, Coach Rupp's health was already noticeably deteriorating—he was about sixty-four at that time. It was often difficult for him to go on trips with me to recruit.

Climbing in and out of private planes, staying overnight in places where he could not sleep well just wore him out. He had gotten to the point where he didn't want to travel any great distance at all if he could avoid it, and he left the recruiting job for Harry and me to do. I did not mind sharing recruiting responsibilities, as my contract stated, but I never wanted the full responsibility. Nevertheless, recruiting was left mainly to me and often kept me away from my home and family.

Sometimes during tight games, Coach Rupp would get nervously confused and frantically ask Harry, then later me, "They're beating us! What should we do? Who should we send in?" At first we would make suggestions. Some of those suggestions improved our situation, but others did not. If we gave good advice, he never gave us any credit on his after-games radio/television programs, but if we lost a game, he would be sure to say something like, "Well, if I hadn't listened to my assistants, we wouldn't have lost that game." He would go on and on. He never assumed any responsibility for his coaching when the team lost. And if we won by a close margin, he'd say, "Well, if I hadn't listened to my assistants, we would have won by a bigger count."

Everyone who knew anything at all about Coach Rupp and our program knew that whoever followed him would have a hard time—not only because of his outstanding record but because he would remain on the sidelines critically watching and talking about everything his successor did or did not do. He would have none of this retiring to Florida to live in a nice condo and bask in the sunshine on a beach sipping his bourbon. No, he would continue to go to his office.

I suffered much stress that year, although I understood the anguish he was experiencing. By 1969, he had been in charge of the program for nearly forty years. He was used to doing things his way, used to giving orders and making requests and having them carried out. Naturally he could not understand why this new president, Singletary, was declaring he would apply the mandatory retirement age of seventy for all university employees, including him. Never short on vanity, he thought of himself as no ordinary employee and therefore the university's mandatory retirement age should not apply to him. He reminded people how exceptional he was, pointing out that no one else had done what he had done. And he was right. No one else had brought such fame to Kentucky basketball. Rupp's fans were devoted to him, and hateful calls from them kept coming, causing much distress to my family.

One afternoon while we were all working in our offices, we heard a disturbance in the hall. It was Coach Rupp berating Harry to someone. Harry overheard him and asked him to step into his office, where he proceeded to blast him for criticizing him. That afternoon, Harry let go of all the suppressed anger he had stifled over the years, letting it all fly out. Coach Rupp was astounded and hurt. After that terrible encounter, their relationship was never the same. They greeted each other politely and talked only about business.

About four or five years later, when Harry learned that Coach Rupp was in the hospital again and that this time he was dying of spinal cancer, he rushed to his old friend's bedside and apologized. Having Harry there with him again made Coach Rupp happy and grateful. That final visit of reconciliation was good for them both, for only a day or so later, on the evening of December 10, 1977, Coach Rupp died. Harry grieved deeply. Often in nostalgic moments later, he would say how much he regretted waiting so long to apologize to his old buddy.

Cosmic forces were at work on that bitter cold night he passed. The team and I were in Kansas playing against his alma mater. Within minutes of our winning that game, Coach Rupp died. We did not get the news until we were on the plane returning home. When the captain announced the news, we all bowed our heads and prayed silently for a few moments. The flight home was a quiet one.

24

The Heir Apparent, 1969–1970

You've got to know when to hold 'em, know when to fold 'em
Know when to walk away, know when to run.

Kenny Rogers

With Harry gone now, I was Coach Rupp's No. 1 assistant, the heir apparent. I felt good about that. I was happy to see how much support I was getting from Wildcat fans, members of the faculty and staff, and even from some of the board members. Albert Clay, the chairman of the board of trustees, was very outspoken about being in favor of my succeeding Coach Rupp. This show of support infuriated Coach Rupp, who had just as many fans, if not more, who were demanding that the university's mandatory age requirement be set aside for him. He treated me as if I were his enemy, and some of his supporters continued to make daily hate phone calls to my wife and children. It was a troubling time for us.

When it was made clear to everyone that Dr. Singletary was going to enforce the mandatory retirement age policy, I went to Coach Rupp and said, "I want you to retire when you want to. I do not want the university to make you retire. But I have no control over what they do. All I want you to do is put in writing what you have already told me, that you recommend I succeed you." He said nothing and turned away. I went to Harry and told him the same. He too refused to put it in writing but said he would support me if I were recommended. Both had told me earlier they would support me for the position, so why would they not say that in writing? To this day, I cannot understand why both refused.

Recommending me publicly as his successor would have

helped not only me but our entire program. For then I could tell my recruits that I would be their coach when Coach Rupp retired in a couple of years. As it was playing out, parents would ask me, "Who is going to be coaching my son? We hear talk that Coach Rupp is going to retire at the end of this year? Next year? What's going to happen? Who is going to be my son's coach?" I could never answer their questions.

I wanted Coach Rupp to do for me what Coach Ed Diddle at Western Kentucky University in Bowling Green in the early 1960s had done for his first assistant John Oldham. Two whole years before he retired, Coach Diddle announced that he wanted John Oldham to be his successor. Doing that allowed Johnny to recruit players who would play for him. He could make a smooth transition and continue to build Western's program. Coach Rupp refused to do the same for me and our program. Why? Your guess is as good as mine.

In 1968, I turned down a job offer to be an assistant to the new head coach, C. M. Newton, at the University of Alabama. Early the next year, I got an invitation from St. Louis University to come for an interview for the head coach position. With a heavy heart I decided to go. I was so stressed out dealing with the daily turmoil going on in our program that I thought the only solution was for me to leave UK.

Before I left that gray morning, I asked Coach Rupp and Harry once more if they would officially support me, and again both said they were in favor of my having the job, but again neither would make a firm commitment by putting it in writing.

So I went to St. Louis, which welcomed me heartily, and signed a contract although there were five stipulations I insisted be added. I stayed in St. Louis for a week setting up my office. During that time, all five of my stipulations were broken. I then returned home on the weekend to make our moving arrangements. I was not happy with the contract with St. Louis, and I was not happy with my situation at UK. I was not happy.

I was working at home that weekend trying to tie things up in preparation for our move when Claude Vaughan, a trainer who was practically Coach Rupp's shadow, phoned me, saying he was driving Coach Rupp to the airport to fly somewhere to give a talk and that Coach Rupp needed to speak to me that very day before he left. He stressed *needed*. Claude asked if I would ride to the airport with them. Wondering what Coach Rupp was up to now, I agreed. Later, Claude would say that I was the one who called him about talking to Coach Rupp, but that is not true.

At the airport, as Claude went to get the luggage checked in, Coach Rupp and I were alone in the backseat of the car. He turned to me and said quietly, "Joe, I want you to come back as my first assistant. I cannot get along without you now. You know the program better than anybody else, and you can help me coach. I need your help, Joe." He sounded so different, almost humble, all of his usual arrogance gone. I looked straight at him. He was a sick, worn-out old man with deep, dark lines in his face, slumped shoulders, and a slight tremor in his hands. I felt sorry for him. Then he said he would that same night officially recommend to the president of the university and to the boards that I be his successor when he retired. I told him I would stay only under those conditions.

My friends Carl Radcliffe, Harry Miller, my attorney, and I left for St. Louis long before daylight that Monday. We arrived early that April morning and met with Father Jerome Marchetti, president of the university. I told him I wanted to be released from my contract because they had reneged on five stipulations that I had insisted on having in my contract. Father Marchetti said he was very sorry, that he had stepped outside his bounds when he told me he could add those five items. He said he had had no authority to do that. He then asked me what I wanted him to do, and I replied, "I want you to release me from this contract." He took his pen and wrote across the front page of the contract, "I hereby release Joe B. Hall from this contract." He signed and dated the document.

The *St. Louis Post-Dispatch* on April 9, 1969, quoted Father

Marchetti as saying, "We were confident that Joe Hall could assist us in developing an outstanding basketball program at St. Louis University. His request for release from his contract came as a complete surprise to us. Under the circumstances, we have honored his request and released him from contract, effective immediately."

Harry, Carl, and I headed home to Lexington. That same day Coach Rupp returned from his trip and met with me and Harry, who had typed a statement for Coach Rupp to read at the press conference that was to be televised that night. I looked Coach Rupp in the eye and said, "I want to know for certain this time if I am going to be the head coach when you retire, and I want you to retire when you are ready to do so. I am in no hurry to have your job! I just want proof that you recommend me to be your successor." I do not know how my request and the reason for it could have been said any plainer.

Coach Rupp promised to make that statement official and public, and he kept his promise. He announced in his press conference that evening, "Now that Joe Hall has returned to Kentucky at my request to be my assistant, and to be named my successor, I am recommending to the athletic board that it appoint Joe B. Hall as my successor within the parameters of their ability to do so according to the framework of its rules and regulations."

It was important to me that Coach Rupp make his announcement publicly—on television—because doing so would finally put an end, I thought and hoped, to some of the false stories that had been circulating.

Later that same year, when Dr. Singletary interviewed him, asking him if he had ever recommended me to be his successor, Coach Rupp answered, "No!" His answer showed that he either did not remember or did not want to admit that he had in fact done so on a television program in April. The television station recorded that program and saved a copy in its files. The television sports director who was present when that recording was made in April was surprised and annoyed when he learned that Coach Rupp had denied to the new UK president that he had ever named me as his successor. Others who knew better too were upset. Although the sports director was no longer working at the station at that time, he instructed his successor where to find the original tape in the station's storage stacks. The new director found the tape and aired it on his nightly TV sports program. I was home watching that program, as I regularly did, when my phone rang. It was Dr. Singletary. "Joe, are you watching television now? Did you hear what Rupp just said?" I answered, "Yes, sir, I did." Dr. Singletary replied, "I cannot believe he lied to me about that promise he had made to you."

25

The Agony, 1971–1972

Adolph saw Joe Hall as his biggest problem that season, I
think. He felt if he could discredit his chief competition it
would be to his advantage. He did not have a kind word to say
about Joe all year.

Harry Lancaster

Those in our department and outside of it saw firsthand how
Adolph tried to run me down and get me out of the eyes of
the public. On his radio and television programs, he made no effort
to conceal his bad feelings toward me. I could do nothing right in
his eyes, although it was obvious I was doing a great deal to help
him retire at the top of his game. He would accuse me of leading a
movement to retire him so I could have his job. It was not unusual
for friends to report his latest accusation. One day Lefty Driesell,
the coach at Maryland, called to tell me, "Joe, Rupp is saying you are
stabbing him in the back!" I replied, "No. That's not true. No one
except Coach Rupp himself would say that. He is the one spreading
that tale." All those I worked with or came in contact with knew
that I had never, ever said anything like that. I always maintained
that he should retire when he was ready to do so.

Coach Rupp refused to acknowledge that the university's
mandatory retirement at seventy was something I had nothing to do
with. Although his behavior was troubling to me and to my family,
I did not take his actions personally. I knew he liked and trusted
me. He had followed me throughout my career from way back in
1948 when I was a student and asked him to help me transfer to
another college where I could play ball. He had the Fabulous Five

then and didn't need me. He did help me transfer to Sewanee where I had wonderful experiences and a great long friendship with Coach Varnell.

He followed my career after that. I received notes and calls from Coach Rupp every now and then. When my Regis team beat Hank Iba's team, he was very impressed and he called to tell me so. He would always congratulate me when I had done something worthy of praise, and I helped him all I could by sending him names of athletes I thought were talented enough to make a significant contribution to his Wildcat team. He and I were friends.

I knew I couldn't take personally what he was trying to do to me while he was being forced out of a career he loved. I believed he would have acted that way toward anyone else who was to follow him. I cannot say what he hoped would happen, but it appeared as if he wanted me to fail.

That last year of his coaching was the hardest on him and on everyone else in the program, for he was more high-strung and temperamental than ever. And he was often out sick and in pain. Even the team was affected somewhat, for the boys, especially those who listened to his radio programs, could not avoid knowing he was characterizing me as a traitor to him. He turned his support to one of his two assistants—Gale Catlett. At one point, he briefly pulled me and one of his assistants out of practice and turned it all over to Gale Catlett. After a little while, Kevin Grevey (I think that's who it was) and some other players met with Coach Rupp and told him they thought they were losing their strength since Coach Catlett had done away with the conditioning program. They knew how important it was that they stay conditioned. Without the running and weightlifting, they told him, they feared they would lose their endurance. He agreed and put me and the other assistant back into practices.

Our first game in the UKIT Christmas tournament was with Missouri, a team in the Big 8 Conference. Coach Rupp assigned Gale Catlett to scout Missouri. Gale had been an assistant coach at

Kansas, so he knew that Missouri team very well because they were in the same conference. We beat Missouri. After that game, Coach Rupp, speaking on his radio program, lavished praise on Coach Catlett for the victory. He added, "Now tomorrow night, we will see what kind of job Joe Hall has done scouting Princeton." My heart sank.

Coached by Pete Carril, Princeton had won the first night, and their final record for that season was 20–7. They had an outstanding player in Brian Taylor, who averaged twenty-five points a game, and three other players who averaged in the double digits. We had never scouted them by themselves, nor had we practiced for them. Although I had watched them play in the game before ours, we had very little time to prepare our team to go against them. I was very worried about that game. I told our center Jim Andrews, "I am on the spot here, Jim." He replied, "We know, Coach, and we will take care of it." And they did take care of it and in a grand fashion too, winning by fourteen points—96–82. I was so proud and thankful for them. On his radio talk show that night, Coach Rupp did not mention me, my scouting, or our victory over Princeton.

Still, I continued to work hard for him. I helped him turn his program around. I got players for him who regained his dominance of the conference that he had lost. Because of the good recruiting, he remained the Baron of Basketball his last seven years of coaching. We had recruited Dan Issel, Mike Pratt, Terry Mills, Tom Parker, Stan Key, Jim Andrews, Larry Stamper, Jim Dinwiddie, and other players of that high caliber.

The seven years *before* I was hired, Kentucky had won only one Southeastern Conference championship and one co-championship in 1962 with Mississippi State. During the seven years *after* I was hired, Kentucky won five Southeastern Conference championships and one co-championship in 1972 with Tennessee. The introduction of the conditioning program and the talented players we recruited contributed to Kentucky's improvement.

Coach Rupp was very ill before Christmas 1971 and was in

and out of the hospital for several weeks. I took over for him on February 12, 1971, and coached the remaining seven games. The first game I was in charge of was an away game with Florida the next day. The day we left the weather was bitterly cold, and our flight there was miserable for a variety of reasons. The boys seemed disgruntled. A few of them were loudly complaining and arguing, and a couple of them got into a fight, upsetting the stewardess. She said she was going to tell the pilot to land the plane, but I asked her to let me first see if I could get things to settle down. I did get the boys calmed down and told them they had to change their attitude so that we could play a good game. Then next thing we knew, the pilot said we were going to land in Georgia to de-ice the plane and spend the night. That was disappointing news and put the boys in a bad mood again. Nothing went right on that trip.

When we finally got to Florida, a day late, we had no time to practice before the game. We lost that first game with Florida, but we won the next six, scoring over one hundred points in five of those six games. We had lost to Tennessee earlier in the season, but we beat them in the last game of the season to win the SEC championship.

After Coach Rupp was released from the hospital, he took over the team again, although he was not feeling well. We lost to Johnny Oldham's Western Kentucky team in the Mideast Regional, and we lost again to Marquette in the consolation game.

Later that same year, when the board of trustees and the athletic board interviewed me about Coach Rupp's competency to coach, I told them that I thought he was competent to continue coaching and that he should be allowed to do so. I said I did not think it was fair to make him retire after all he had done for basketball, for the University of Kentucky, and for the Commonwealth as a whole. I told them, "An exception should be made for him because of his remarkable career. He is entitled to be treated differently and allowed to make his own decision about his retirement." And I had said all those same things earlier to him and to all the others with whom I spoke. No one can say that I did not stand up for him, or that I was not loyal to him right to the end.

When board members asked me questions about his drinking alcohol in his office, I said I had never seen him do it, and I had not. Coach Rupp had never made it a secret that he loved bourbon; newspaper reporters and others had already written about it. They knew too he was no heavy drinker, no alcoholic, and none of them made him out to be one. I never saw him drunk or even heard of him being drunk.

Whenever we traveled for games, he would always have Harry keep him well stocked with fifths of bourbon, beer, and snacks for his after-the-game gatherings in his hotel room. He loved those times and looked forward to them. After a game, he would change into his red pajamas and then welcome people to come to his room to have a few drinks and something to eat while they rehashed the game with him.

I don't believe he ever drank at school until his last two years, after the retirement issue emerged. Around that time, I was told that he had started keeping a bottle of vodka (because it is odorless) in his desk drawer along with several packages of chewing gum. Toward closing time each day, he may have had a "little toddy." At school, the managers had always provided him with dozens of packages of Wrigley's Juicy Fruit, for he always chewed gum during games. Later, he believed that chewing gum masked the alcohol on his breath. After having his little afternoon refreshment, he would pop three or four pieces of gum in his mouth, chew noisily, and then come up beside me and blow in my face, asking, "Hey, Joe, my breath smells good, huh?" "Yeah, Coach, it does." And we both would laugh.

I have always been grateful for Coach Rupp, for he gave me the greatest opportunity of my life—to come back to Kentucky, my home, and be a coach at the school that I loved. He chose me because he had confidence that I could do his job, believing in my achievements as a coach. Why would I ever bad-mouth him?

The truth is I never did, not even to my closest friends or family. I respected his achievements too much, and also I knew another side to him. Although he sometimes acted angry, and he put on good shows of anger, I never saw him truly angry. He was just being *Coach* Rupp. I knew him to be a good family man, devoted to his wife, whom he used to call jokingly "the War Department," and to Herky, their son and only child.

I knew too that Coach Rupp had a big heart. When he learned that Harry's mother had died while Harry was in New Orleans scouting at the Sugar Bowl, Coach Rupp made and paid for all the arrangements for Harry to return home immediately before he called to tell his friend the sad news. A few times he gave money to some kid so he could fly home when there was an illness or a death in his family. He had a deep compassion for sick children. Until he became too ill himself, he was the major fundraiser for the Shriners, and he raised enormous sums for the Shriners Hospitals for Children.

Those chewing outs and hard times he gave me and others were just part of his "routine" to remind us he was in charge. He always had to be in charge. True, there were occasions when his tantrums were hurtful or annoying, but more often than not we were amused by them. I am grateful to have had Adolph Rupp in this wonderful life I have lived.

26

UK Head Coach, 1972

Never be the man who follows The Man. Remember that
advice. And then remember to nod your head in admiration
toward Joe B. Hall because he not only was the man who
followed The Man, he was the man who did it well.

Rick Bozich

On the afternoon of April 28, 1972, Dr. Otis Singletary was
going to announce at a televised press conference that Adolph
Rupp's mandatory retirement had taken effect, and that by the
board of trustee's unanimous decision I was officially the head
coach of the University of Kentucky basketball team. I was forty-
three years old and about to take on the biggest challenge of my life.
For forty-two years, the only basketball coach many people knew
was Adolph Rupp. Because of him Kentucky is famous not only for
Thoroughbred horses and bourbon, but also for basketball. Many
people were wondering if I would be capable of taking his place.

When it was time for me to leave for the meeting, I put on
my suit coat, brushed my hair, and headed across the campus to the
Office Tower where the meeting was to be held. Television and radio
people had already set up their equipment and a crowd had gathered.
It so happened that Dr. Singletary was getting on the elevator the
same time I was. We talked pleasantly about generalities, got off the
elevator, and walked the remaining stairs to the top floor.

As we were about to enter the large conference room, he said to
me, "Joe, we haven't discussed your salary." I said, "Dr. Singletary,
that was settled when I came back from St. Louis. We didn't have a
president at that time and, acting for the president as the chairman

of the board of trustees, Albert Clay told me that my salary would be the same as Coach Rupp's—$65,000." Dr. Singletary looked surprised and said, "Well, that will never be! Your salary will be $20,000." Shaken by his answer, and remembering the $40,000 I had turned down at St. Louis, I said, "Dr. Singletary, are you serious?" He looked at me and said firmly, "If you want this job, the salary is $20,000. Now do we hold this press conference or not?" I was sick with disappointment and anger, but said quietly, "Go for it." What should have been one of the sweetest days of my life had turned sour quickly.

I had suspected that Dr. Singletary would present an obstacle for me because he was not interested in basketball. He had no idea what basketball had done for Kentucky and how many people supported and loved the Wildcats. He had worked at Louisiana State University and came to us from Texas A&M, and both Louisiana and Texas were strong football states. Basketball in Texas then was considered a minor sport. Soon after he arrived in August 1969, it was obvious he had brought his passion for football to Kentucky. He arrived on our campus right at the time Coach Rupp was creating a lot of turmoil about being forced to retire. Singletary saw the old man as a thorn in his side, and thus had another reason to ignore basketball.

Coach Rupp was not present at this press conference. Someone said he left his office shortly before the program was to start, saying he was going to his farm. He had not sent any congratulatory words to be read to me. After the announcement, I immediately returned to my same small office. Coach Rupp was permitted to continue using his large office, only the sign on his door had been changed to "Consultant."

Try to imagine the intense pressure I felt as I began my career as head coach following a living legend—*the winningest coach in the nation*. Yet I was looking forward to the challenge of keeping the Kentucky program competitive. I embraced that awesome responsibility.

Try to imagine, too, how it was to have Coach Rupp still coming to his office almost daily, seeing me, the players, and my staff. He had every right to do that, of course, but his being there made things more difficult for me and for the players, who felt an unspoken pressure from his presence. He also kept his television and radio programs, regularly commenting on the games.

As usual, we had a tough schedule. Fortunately, I had a good team led by two strong seniors, Jim Andrews and Larry Stamper, and our junior guard, Ronnie Lyons. I relied heavily on Andrews and Stamper for their leadership roles. Andrews especially was a mature young man with good judgment who saw to it that the sophomores, who were typically but not seriously mischievous, followed the rules. He and Larry did some mentoring that year.

I felt good about my sophomores. I had recruited many of them and had coached them their freshman year. They ended their season with an ideal record, 22–0. As freshmen, they were so talented they were called the Super Kittens. You will recognize their names, for they went on to become rather famous. They are Bob Guyette, Kevin Grevey, Jerry Hale, Mike Flynn, Steve Lochmueller, Jimmy Dan Conner, and G. J. Smith.

The first game I coached as head coach was an exhibition game with the Chilean National team, which we won easily, 125–62.

We opened our regular season on the road against Michigan State, a team that had beaten Coach Rupp's the year before. We won that game 75–66. We played good defense that time. Unlike Coach Rupp, who used only eight players, I played all twelve men. The Kentucky fans took favorable note of that.

Then my good luck vanished. Our next game was at home in Memorial Coliseum against Iowa. Coach Rupp, with a bag of popcorn, sat on the bench behind me in a spectator's seat. I was so preoccupied with all I had to do that I cannot remember now what or even if he said anything to me. He, too, must have been deep in his own thoughts. It had to have been painful for him to be there. It was the first time in forty-two years that he was not coaching the

Wildcats—something he had wanted to do until he died. I believe he would have preferred dropping dead on the court to sitting in a spectator's seat watching someone else coach his team.

Much to my regret, we lost that game. For those who like to keep accounts of such records, it was the first time in ten years that UK had lost a home-opener game and only the third time in forty-six years. I have no words to describe how miserable I felt about that fact. It gave such ammunition to those who said that I would fail in trying to follow Coach Rupp.

As if that loss was not bad enough, we went on to lose to Indiana 64–58 on their floor, and we lost again to North Carolina by nineteen points in Freedom Hall in Louisville. At a point in that NC game, I got so upset with the official that instead of ripping his head off, I ripped off my coat as I yelled my objections to his call. My emotions spilled out. I slammed my coat on the floor and was stamping on it when one of my players, Jimmy Dan Conner, grabbed and restrained me. My players had never seen me behave that way. Those who know me know that it is not my nature to display such anger, such emotion, but that night I just could not tolerate watching my boys keep missing the basket. Here I had been given the best freshman team in the country, and the scoreboard showed I was not coaching them well. I turned to Dick Parsons, my assistant, and said despairingly, "Dick, go set a fire in a wastepaper basket! Let's do something so we can get out of here!"

I was losing my confidence in my ability to coach, and coaching was never something I had worried about before. I made up my mind that night I would quit coaching if I could not get my team to play any better than they were doing. I had been so successful coaching at a high school, and then successful again for six years at Regis, a small college. It had never occurred to me that I would have problems coaching, but that's what the trouble appeared to be because I had talented players. When Coach Rupp hired me as his assistant, I worried about being in that bright spotlight that always shines intensely on UK basketball, not my coaching. But here I was losing three out of our first four games. Man, that hurts, that's gut-wrenching—even still after all these years.

My players saw my distress and put more effort forth. But their own confidence had been shaken too. In our next two games, Andrews, Grevey, and Conner went into a scoring spree, and the freshmen played well too. By beating Nebraska and Oregon we won the UKIT. We won our games over Kansas and Notre Dame but lost to Mississippi in our first SEC road game. Mississippians went wild with joy, for it was the first time they had beaten a UK basketball team in forty-five years. With every loss, we broke some kind of record, and that compounded my misery. We went on to lose three more conference games but still won the SEC Conference championship by beating Tennessee. That victory made us very happy. At the end of that game, the players lifted me up on their shoulders and carried me to the locker room.

In the Mideast Regional of the NCAA, we beat Austin Peay in the first round, but lost to Indiana in the finals.

The next year, our 1973–1974 season, which I had so optimistically looked forward to, turned out to be one of my worst. That season was a gut check! I don't know what you'd call it, other than a lousy year. We had a very tough schedule, and we no longer had tall players compared to our competition's team. We lost Jim Andrews, and we moved Guyette to center, Conner to forward, Ronnie Lyons to guard.

The last game of our season was to be the last played in Memorial Coliseum, for Rupp Arena was under construction. However, several years later, one other game was played in it because of a conflict in scheduling. With our 12–13 record, I was deeply concerned about how we would perform. If we lost this one, we would be the first UK basketball team since 1926 to end the season with a losing record. As it turned out, we finished much better than I had feared. After being ten down in the second half, Mississippi

State player Rich Knarr, during a break, shocked everyone when he leaned into Cawood Ledford's broadcasting microphone and shouted, "Hey, Mom! We've beaten Kentucky!"

I told the boys what Rich Knarr had just said and that lit a fire in them. We came back strong and tied the game in regulation and beat Mississippi State by one point in overtime. Surely, the spirits of past Wildcats had helped us win the last game we played in the grand old Memorial Coliseum. We managed to close the season at 13–13, matching Coach Rupp's 1966–1967 record of 13–13.

After that disappointing season, I had to do something special to raise my boys' spirits and give them more confidence. They had all worked hard and done everything that I asked them to do. I remembered what a great experience it had been for me when I was their age to go with Coach Varnell and his basketball team on the European tour. I thought, "That's it! I'll take my boys on a foreign tour."

27

Australian Tour, 1974

Travel and change of place impart a new vigor of the mind.

Seneca

The summer of 1974 was memorable. Once I had the idea of traveling abroad, I sent letters to basketball federations all over the world. Lindsay Gaze, coach of the Australian team, responded with a suggested series of games and offered to cover all expenses for our tour.

After I had all the information, I called the boys in and surprised them by telling them we were going to travel abroad. They were so happy to get this news. Then I asked them how long they wanted to stay. Jimmy Dan Conner spoke right up, saying, "We want to stay three months. We want to stay all summer!" I told him, "Jimmy Dan, you would not be happy staying that long in a foreign place, living out of a suitcase, eating strange foods, playing games every day and traveling in buses every day. No, we will stay two weeks." When he pleaded again, I gave in and agreed we'd stay a month.

We left May 12 and returned June 7. On our way over, we stopped in Tahiti overnight and played their national team and won. The next morning our host gave us a tour of the island. At one point, we stopped at a service station. After a short rest, we loaded up again to continue the tour. In a matter of minutes, a horrified Cliff Hagan (our athletic director) suddenly realized his son was missing. The driver turned around and went back to find the little boy standing in front of the station waiting. Cliff was so relieved, and so were we all.

Early that afternoon we boarded a plane to Australia where we played nineteen games in twenty-six days and lost only two. Each town had its own team but would draw All Stars from other teams to boost its roster. I remember one of the Stars, a native Australian, was a student at LSU. It was a grueling trip, traveling each morning to a different town and arriving just in time to get dressed to play a game. Nevertheless, it toughened the boys up for the season to come.

At one of the games during a half-time, I was leaning over the scorer's table talking to someone when I felt a pull on my coat tail. I turned and saw this tiny old man, not even five feet tall. He whispered to me, "The refs are going *to pinch* the game." I never found out what "pinch" meant but figured it wasn't good.

For our housing arrangements, we had *billets*. Individual families in each town volunteered to pick the boys up after a game and take them to their homes for meals and overnight stays, then return them to our meeting place the next morning. Each night, the billets would tell us where we would be playing the next day.

Dick Parsons, my assistant, Cliff Hagan, the athletic director, and Dr. V. A. Jackson, the team physician, went with us. We stayed in hotels and each of us had our own room. I took Steve, my son, and Cliff took his son, Chip. Dick drove the boys in a large vehicle of some kind but I cannot remember what kind; Cliff and I each had a car. Dr. Jackson rode with me.

Driving in Australia was a scary experience for me because they drive on the left side of the road. It was nerve-racking for me to lead our other vehicles through heavy traffic on the "wrong" side of the road. Turning right in busy traffic was a nightmare.

Although our tour was during our summer, it was winter in Australia and freezing cold. The gyms were sometimes uncomfortably cold, for they were not heated. The fans wore overcoats and blankets. Even barbers in their shops would wear overcoats. In the hotel, all we had was a little electric bar that glowed red and gave off some heat. The Australians are very hearty people.

We traveled all the way across the outback to get to Adelaide on the west coast. We passed through a section that is Australia's horse country, and we saw many Thoroughbred horse farms and also some wineries. All the cattle farms grew eucalyptus trees. The leaves on these trees are full of moisture, and during droughts the farmers would feed the leaves to their cattle. Some sections of the country are heavily populated, but not the part called the outback. As we drove through it, we were hoping to see some wild kangaroos but we never saw any along the roads. We did see plenty of them in the parks. There were rumors that they would jump your car as you drove down the highway.

The Australians we met were good-natured and friendly. We enjoyed being with them. I remember too how much they loved our movies, and how delicious the food was in the taverns. They had a law that required any place that served alcoholic beverages to also serve food and to have rooms available for overnight stays. It was the custom then for many men, after they got off work at the end of the day, to go to a tavern to have a beer, socialize, perhaps eat, and if they chose to do so spend the night.

While the boys were dining with the families with whom they were billeted, we ate at the taverns, where the food was very good. We found one particular place that served the best lamb stew I have ever eaten. They had it simmering in a huge black kettle that was sitting on the bar counter, and alongside it was a dipper, clean bowls, and spoons. We could serve ourselves and go back for seconds. That Australian lamb stew at that place was divine. I like beef too, but their beef was all grass-fed, so it had very little fat. Sure, it is healthier that way, but not nearly as tasty.

After each game, we would stand in the parking lot, waiting for the families with whom the players were billeted to pick them up. One night toward the end of our two-week stay while we were waiting in the parking lot, I kept feeling some little hits on my back. I turned around and there was Jimmy Dan Conner with a mournful expression on his face and a handful of pebbles. I said, "Jimmy Dan, what are you doing?" He answered softly, "Coach, let's go home."

I reminded him, "Jimmy Dan, you are the reason we are stuck here for two more weeks. Do you realize that? You wanted us to stay all summer, and I said no—two weeks is enough. Do you remember that? Then you complained again, and I gave in to you and agreed to stay a month. Remember that, do you? So cheer up, buddy!"

We had gained valuable experience from our Australian trip, winning seventeen of nineteen games, and when we returned 1974–1975 was one of my very best seasons. I had a taller squad with the addition of what we called our twin towers—Rick Robey and Mike Phillips, both at six feet, ten inches. We also had Grevey, six feet five, as forward, and we had two good-sized guards in Mike Flynn, six feet three, and Conner, six feet four. We still had Bob Guyette, six feet eight, as forward. My bench was strong with senior Jerry Hale and two more freshmen: James Lee, six feet six, and Jack Givens, six feet five. This team had an abundance of ability in shooting, defense, depth, speed, and size.

We started our season by beating Northwestern and Miami of Ohio. After having a humiliating defeat at Indiana, 98–74, we went on to beat North Carolina, then won the UKIT, and we beat Kansas and Notre Dame before starting the SEC schedule. We lost three games in the SEC to finish as co-champions, which sent us to the NCAA Mideast Regional where we defeated Marquette and advanced to the Elite Eight in Dayton, Ohio. We defeated Central Michigan in the first game, leaving us to face undefeated, No. 1 ranked Indiana for the right to advance to the Final Four.

28

The Avengers! 1975

Victory is sweetest when you've known defeat.

Malcolm Forbes

On December 7, 1974, when the Hoosiers defeated us on their home floor in my third regular season, they were a veteran club, ranked No. 1 in the nation, and had most of their starters from the year before. We had lost four key players and were coming off a 13–13 season. We were not even ranked in the AP Poll. We were returning with sophomores, one senior, and two freshmen. We were depending on youth without experience. Yet we played probably one of the best and most physical games that I ever coached. The emotions were out of sight. We had fought the opposition pretty evenly, but their depth and experience wore us down. We were totally outlasted and lost by twenty-four points.

In the final moments of the game, the referee called a foul against Indiana's Steve Alford for running into our boy Jerry Hale. That call made Bobby Knight apoplectic! He had already been fuming because he thought too many fouls had been called on his team. He couldn't bear having another foul—even though his team was way, way ahead of us. While Hale was shooting his free throws in front of our bench—that was our offensive end of the court—Bobby rushed all the way down in front of our bench to argue with the official. This was before the NCAA established a restriction line on how far coaches could travel down the sidelines. He was standing there in front of our bench giving the official his typical loud, venomous, Bobby Knight treatment.

Now before I tell you the rest of this story, I have to tell you this part first. For years, Bobby and I had been good friends. We had spent a week fishing together in Wyoming. When we coached together in Colorado at the Olympic trials under Hank Iba, we had dinner together and went to a movie every night while we were there. We were friends—or so I thought. Now let's go back to that game.

After yelling at the official, he turned to go back to his bench. As he passed in front of me, I good-naturedly said to him, "Way to go, Bobby—give 'em hell!" He stopped in his tracks, spun around, and stooped in an aggressive crouched position. He pointed his finger at my face and yelled, "Don't you ever talk to me during a game. Coach your own m——f—— team." I was shocked.

I felt that I needed to apologize to him, so I walked up to the scorer's table and explained, "Bobby, don't be upset with me. I didn't mean anything by that. You have a great team! You kicked our butts soundly. You are going to have a great year." He did not reply or even look at me. As I turned to walk away, he sprang up and flipped me hard on the back of my head with his open hand. Stunned, I asked, "What was that for?" He answered sarcastically, "Well, I didn't mean anything by that either."

There I was with a twenty-four-point deficit, facing all of our players, a packed stadium, and a nationwide television audience, being humiliated and slapped on my head by someone I thought was my friend, who was upset over some trivial thing I had said jokingly. I was angry but I knew I had to control my emotions. I had just taken a terrible loss, and it would make me look like a sore loser if I hit him back—which I wanted so badly to do. Although it took everything in me to do so, I remained calm. My assistant Lynn Nance, a karate expert, was by my side wanting to take Bobby on. My other assistants, Dick Parsons and Leonard Hamilton, had also rushed to my defense. I said, "We all have to calm down as best we can. Now let's go back to our bench and finish playing this nightmare."

After the game ended, the Indiana athletic director walked over to me and said, "Joe, you and Bobby walk off the court together to show there is no problem." Bobby came over and stuck his head in our conversation in time to hear me say, "The only place I will walk with Bobby Knight is behind the stands to kick his ass." Bobby scoffed, gave me the finger, and ran off the court. If I had cold-cocked him as I wanted so badly to do, I would have said to him what he said to me, "I didn't mean anything by that, Bobby. We're good friends."

After that exchange, our relationship was never the same. After I retired from coaching and was doing television color commentary for ABC, I went to Bloomington once to call a game for him. The day before that game, I went to watch his practice and interview him. He invited Gary Bender and me to go to dinner with him that evening and on to Noblesville to see his son play. It was all very awkward. Throughout the years, I would occasionally see him at various games, but we never talked. He has never apologized to me.

There have been other instances when Bobby Knight performed like a first-class jerk. You may recall that time when he threw a chair across the floor during half-time in a game. He explained to reporters afterward something like this: "As I was leaving at half-time, I saw this elderly lady standing. I thought she could use a chair, so I threw her one." That's what he told the press!

I have always been inclined to believe in the Hindu concept of karma, which maintains that doing good deeds will bring us blessings and success, while doing bad deeds will bring us misery and harm. The old saying is "What goes around, comes around!" I felt karma's presence the next time we played Indiana.

After Bobby's boys had beaten us, they went undefeated the whole year and were ranked No. 1 and the odds-on favorite to win the NCAA championship when we faced them again in the Mideast Regional Finals on March 22, 1975, in Dayton, Ohio.

We had not forgotten how rough that December game had been played and how Coach Knight behaved like a middle-school bully. My boys were ready and eager to pay them back! We had learned from that last game to be more physical, aggressive, and tough. We had a great bench now too. We were looking forward to facing them.

The night of the game, I went into the locker room to meet with the team. Without saying a word, I walked in and wrote in big letters on the blackboard these four words—Net, Bus, Police, Coliseum. The kids sat staring at the board and then at me, puzzled. I told them: "Boys, we are going to beat Indiana tonight. In our excitement about winning, we have got to be very careful cutting down the net after our victory. I do not want anyone to get hurt or the backboard or anything else damaged. I want you to use a ladder and scissors in cutting down the net. You are all to ride home on the bus together with me. I do not want anyone to ride with friends or even with their parents. We are to stay together on the bus. After we cross the bridge over the Ohio River into Kentucky, we will be met by the Kentucky State Police, who will escort us home to Lexington and on to the Coliseum."

And that's exactly how it all happened. In a nail-biting, jaw-chewing, excitingly close game, we beat Bobby Knight's Indiana 92–90! That victory was so, so sweet. We were all very happy.

I had not called the state police to ask them to lead us, but I had talked to Cawood Ledford on his radio show after the game. I told him what I had said to the boys before the game about their winning, about writing the four words on the blackboard and what they meant. I said too that I hoped the state police were listening to the program. Cawood replied, "Don't worry about it. I will cross the bridge doing ninety if I have to and make sure the state police will be there."

The state police must have been listening to the program because they were there waiting for us in their cruisers when we crossed into Kentucky. The players were excited to see them waving to us as they pulled out in front of our bus to escort us home.

Police escort—yes, maybe, but I never expected to see the number of people standing alongside the highway waving to us! Some had signs and others had flags. They were all waving to us, throwing kisses, and cheering us as we passed by. We had not even imagined people would do anything like that. Traveling behind us were miles of cars with their lights on, honking their horns! I wish I could describe the kind of thrill it is to receive that kind of support, and we got it every place we passed through. When we got to Georgetown, the sheriff there followed the state police cars leading the bus. When we got to Fayette County, our county sheriff there joined us as well and led us to the campus where the campus police escorted us to the Coliseum.

It was hard to hold back the tears when we walked into the Coliseum and saw it jam-packed with fans chanting, "San Diego, here we come!" So many wonderful things happened to me during my coaching career, but the memory of that one night is one I will never forget. I don't think the boys will either.

Naturally, the 1978 championship is more important in defining my career, but the 1975 victory over undefeated Indiana, which was ranked No. 1, was the most exciting and satisfying of my coaching career. To have a team and coaches respond collectively, totally committed and determined, physically and mentally, to achieve a single goal is the ultimate reward for any coach.

Mike Flynn played brilliantly and refused to let his rival Quinn Buckner stop him. Mike was rewarded by leading the team in cutting down the nets. Kevin Grevey gave another superb effort. Jimmy Dan Conner, playing even above his usual toughness, challenged Kent Benson in the chest-bumping body check. Bob Guyette took many charges, and the rest of the team took note of what the officials had told us about handling moving screens, which were standard plays used by Indiana. The officials had told me there was no offensive foul if the defense stopped and no contact followed.

The Kentucky defense, including Robey, Phillips, Givens, and

Lee, put many illegal moving screeners on their backsides, skidding across the hardwood floor. It added to my gratification to win such a hard-fought and meaningful victory.

Bobby Knight ran off the floor that night without the usual good sportsmanship handshake coaches always make.

To that group of young men and the entire squad, I offer my eternal respect and appreciation for giving Kentucky the most meaningful victory in its storied basketball history. Mike Flynn, Kevin Grevey, Jimmy Dan Conner, Jack Givens, James Lee, Bob Guyette, Rick Robey, Mike Phillips, Larry Johnson, Dan Hall, and Merion Haskins—these were my valiant young Wildcats who kept Indiana from having a perfect season and who paved our way to San Diego, to the Final Four in 1975!

One of the best scorers anywhere, Kevin Grevey, has written that he and the other seniors thought the Indiana game was the most important one they ever played, and many sports enthusiasts agree.

The game made *USA Today*'s list of the greatest NCAA tournament games of all time (Mike Douchant, "Greatest 63 Games in NCAA Tournament History," the Sports Xchange, *USA Today*, March 25, 2002).

In his July 27, 2018, list of the fifty greatest UK basketball wins of all time, *Lexington Herald-Leader* writer Mark Story ranks this Indiana–Kentucky 1975 game first. He explains that he "tried to rank the games that, as stand-alone entities, were the most compelling."

Robert Marcus wrote in the *Chicago Tribune:*

It took the Slaughterhouse Five to end Indiana's dream of glory. The Kentucky Wildcats played like five guys who make their living sledge hammering steers in a stockyard Saturday to earn their greatest basketball victory in decades. It is unlikely that any other team or any other style could have managed the awesome job. There was a touch of madness to Kentucky's method. This was a team driven by anger and revenge. These twin passions—plus a pair of hot-shooting guards—were too much for even the unbeaten Hoosiers, all year long the top-ranked in the country and the favorite to win the NCAA crown. This was not a typical Kentucky basketball team. You do not expect to get butchered on the boards when you play Kentucky. You expect them to go around and over you, not right through you. (Quoted in Russell Rice, *Kentucky Basketball: The Big Blue Machine*, 394–95.)

29

John Wooden's Ploy: NCAA, 1975

You have no choices about how you lose, but you do have a
choice about how you come back and prepare to win.

Pat Riley

O n our way to San Diego to play in the NCAA championship, I
sat thinking how blessed I was to be going where I was going,
doing what I always wanted to do, and accompanied by a deep and
talented team. I had All-American Kevin Grevey, a senior, who had
averaged 23.6 points per game that season and was shooting better
than 51 percent of his shots. I had Jimmy Dan Conner, another
senior, who averaged 12 points a game; Rick Robey, six foot ten,
a freshman, who scored 10 points a game; and Jack Givens, who
could make 9 points on average. In fact, it would be Jack who saved
us from losing to Syracuse in the semi-final game. With two tough
reserves, Mike Phillips and James Lee, and two more talented
seniors, Bob Guyette and Mike Flynn, I felt confident that we stood
a great chance to win this championship.

We were all excited about being in San Diego. None of the
players had been there before, and they were looking forward to the
visit. That weekend we arrived, we did as much sightseeing as we
could do in the limited amount of time we had. The San Diego Zoo,
the largest in the world, impressed us the most. The next morning,
Easter Sunday, our hotel prepared us a fabulous breakfast and the
coaches' wives surprised us with an Easter egg hunt. A local priest
held a worship service for us. We were relaxed somewhat, though
our big game was tomorrow evening.

The only drawback was how far California is from Kentucky;
many of our fans and even some of the team's own families could

not afford to make the long trip. One of our players, Jack Givens, was happy to have his mother there. Her coworkers in Lexington had all chipped in and raised money for her to make the trip.

We were deep in Bruin territory, and not having our usual large vocal fan base cheering us from the stands concerned us. We figured the entire state was rooting for UCLA to win, although we had heard a little talk about some Californians getting tired of seeing Wooden win every time.

On that Sunday afternoon the day before the game came unexpected news at the press meeting. Bruins coach John Wooden dramatically and officially announced, "After this game, I am retired!" His words struck me like a thunderbolt, and the audience moaned. My assistants and I, and everyone else in the room, knew well what a powerful influence his retirement announcement would have on his players and on his fans, and also maybe on the officials. I felt as if I had lost the game right then and there. I mumbled sarcastically, "And, oh, yeah, my seniors Conner, Flynn, Guyette, Hale, and Smith are going to retire after the game too."

The next day, it seemed as if everybody in California wanted to see John Wooden win his last championship. With nine NCAA championship trophies already on his shelf, he had to have that tenth one to end his coaching career. And he intended to win it, too. He knew well that he could get a motivational edge by making his announcement before the game—not after. And there was not a single thing I could do about it.

As the officials were preparing to start, it was clear to us that the stadium and the Bruins were determined to get that tenth championship for their beloved old coach. Even the referees asked us at the start not to let things get "too rough." As we soon saw throughout the game, they gave Wooden lots of slack on close calls. We played a good game too, but early on, Robey and Phillips got in foul trouble. We took an early six-point lead, but UCLA caught up, and from then on we seesawed points back and forth. Grevey scored eighteen points in the first half and ten in the second.

With less than six minutes left to play, we were only one point behind, at 76–75. UCLA's Dave Meyers went up for a jump shot and missed. He came down on top of Grevey, knocking him to the floor and falling on top of him. When Hank Nichols, the referee, called a foul on him, Meyers yelled, "Dammit!" as he slapped his hand on the floor, and then the referee called a technical on him. So Grevey went to the free-throw line with a one on one (the chance to make two points) plus a technical, which would have given him one point and given us possession of the ball out of bounds. This was our chance to score five points if Grevey made his one on one and the technical and we scored on the possession. And he was a great free-throw shooter, too, so our hopes were high at this point. But Wooden became unhinged and went ballistic. He ran out onto the floor, yelling to the referee, "You crook!" The other referee was trying to stand in front of him as Wooden kept trying to get around him. The referee had him by his elbow, begging him, "Please, please, Mr. Wooden, go back to your bench!" He stubbornly refused. The crowd went crazy!

Grevey, who was standing there waiting for Bob Woodward, the official, to give him the ball so he could make his shots, got a bit unnerved, naturally, as he listened to the coach's tirade, the referee's pleas, and the screaming crowd. I got angry and walked to the scorer's table and yelled, "Let him shoot his free throws!" The official who kept trying to control Wooden heard me and, with the most hateful expression, pointed his finger at me and angrily said, "You go back to your bench, and if you say one more word, I will call a technical foul!" It was at that very moment, when I looked at his face, that I realized how severely Wooden's retirement announcement had affected the outcome of the game. As a third-year UK coach with a great team, I had had high hopes of winning my first NCAA championship that night. Sadly, though, Wooden's six little words had swept all those hopes away in a flash.

When Wooden, still fussing, returned to his bench, the noise from the crowd was unbearable. Yes, dear readers, these were the distracting and deplorable conditions under which we played the national finals.

Grevey, poor kid, was so shook up he missed all his free throws, ones that he would have made in normal circumstances. We got the ball out of bounds and the official called a foul on James Lee for a moving screen violation. We did not get anything out of the foul or the technical. UCLA beat us in the finals by seven points.

All I can say is the boys and I would have liked to play that game with the Bruins again, under different circumstances.

Wooden's ploy bothered all of us, but it affected Kevin Grevey the most. He has talked about it and described his feelings in his book *The Game of My Life*. He writes that Wooden's choice to announce his retirement before the game "was a selfish thing. He chose to do it because he knew it would motivate his players to work extra hard to win." Kevin notes that he had been taught not to put your personal needs before your team's. "He [Wooden] took the spotlight and put it on himself before his team played in the championship and that's not what I as a member of a team was taught [to do]. You don't call attention to yourself." Although Kevin thought Wooden's teachings were worthy, he was disappointed to see that in real life the famous coach did not practice what he preached.

A few years after that game, Kevin happened to be on the same flight with John Wooden. He told him that although he admired him, he was bothered still by what the coach did. He told Wooden that if he had not announced his retirement before the game, UK would have won that championship. He said Wooden smiled and said quietly, "And if you had played a little defense in that game, UK would have probably beat us" (quoted in Denny Trease and Ryan Clark, *Kentucky Wildcats: Tales from the Locker Room*, 74).

Many sportswriters and fans agreed with Kevin. For example, Bill Tanton, sports editor for the *Baltimore Evening Sun*, wrote in his March 31, 1975, article "Wooden Pulls an Ara—And He'll Need It":

After the [semi-final] game, UCLA coach John Wooden announced he is finally retiring after 27 seasons. Thus, tonight's game with Kentucky will be Wooden's 1,008th and last. "I don't want this to be used as a type of hyping anything up for the championship game," Wooden says, "I prefer a workmanlike job."

The words sound nice, John, but the timing betrays you. If you're not interested in hyping, why announce it now—as you go into a game being played for a national championship? If you really want "a workmanlike job" tonight, why not announce your retirement after the season?

Why not? I'll tell you why not. Because Wooden is much too smart to pass up on a chance like this—especially in a big game like tonight's.

30

Running the Wall

Winners embrace hard work. They love the discipline of it, the trade-off they're making to win. Losers, on the other hand, see it as punishment. And that's the difference.

Lou Holtz

We were in Mississippi, sitting in a bus, waiting for three players—LaVon Williams, Freddie Cowan, and Dwane Casey—so we could go to practice. It was a few minutes past the time I had said we were leaving. I hate tardiness, and all my players knew that. A player being late is killing time for the rest of us who are on time. No team should be disturbed by anyone being late. The longer I have to wait, the madder I get. Even though I could see the three of them rushing out the front door of the motel, I told the bus driver to shut the doors and take off. We left them as they were running toward us. They had to get a cab to the gym. Later, as a coach himself, Dwane Casey said that I taught him a lesson that he'll never forget and that he adopted my policy on tardiness with his teams.

Another time, we drove off without Kevin Grevey, an important starter. He called a cab and told the driver to hurry, that he needed to be at that school's gym to play in a basketball game. The cab driver laughed, saying, "You must not be a very important player, if your coach took the team and left without you!"

My punishment for players when they broke a rule or did something wrong in practice was to "run a wall." That meant that a player had to run up the stairs in Memorial Coliseum all the way to the second bleachers and touch the wall, then run down. My first year using that penalty, Larry Stamper fell running down the steps, but he was not hurt. Still, I worried that someone might get hurt. After his fall, I told the others to run up but walk down. It was maybe seventy or so steps. It was a good conditioner, plus a good penalty.

Depending on what the offense was, a player might have to run one or as many as ten walls. If I got really mad, as I did one time after one player made a grievous mistake, I told him to run every step in the Coliseum. He did not have to run them all at one time. He could take two or three days if he needed to, but he was not going to practice until he had run them all. He did it.

I was strict with the boys. Another time—and I don't remember what I had gotten upset over, wish I did, but it was something really serious—I made them all run ten walls before we practiced. Now, that was really a tough penalty, but as I said I was really mad at them. I had the manager charting each player as he came down to the floor. After a player stepped down on the floor, that was one wall. Now, whether he actually touched the wall at the top, I did not know.

After watching James Lee, I saw that he was not coming all the way to the floor on his return. He stopped at the railing of the first section, turned around, and ran back up the stairs. Each time, he was skipping about five or six steps from the floor. I asked the manager how many walls James Lee had done. He said ten. I told him he had done none because he had not touched the floor. James Lee got mad and said he quit the team. He walked away.

That night, his father called me and asked why his son had quit basketball. His son had told him he had quit the team because although he had already run ten walls, I insisted he hadn't. His father was a fine man, the preacher of the largest black church in Lexington. Reverend Lee asked, "Coach Hall, what did James do to make you upset with him?" I told him James was cheating, he was running only partial walls while the other boys were running the wall correctly. Surprised, he asked, "You mean the whole team had to run the wall?" "Yes, sir, the whole team." Reverend Lee said, "Coach Hall, if you will let James Lee come back, he will run the walls." So James Lee returned the next day and ran his ten walls.

After we moved to Rupp Arena, where the walls are a lot farther up than Memorial's, running the wall took too much of my practice time. So I decided that if I were going to continue to have the wall penalty, I would have them run only half of the stairs, to the top of first tier of steps. Unless a player committed a more serious offense, he had to run only one wall.

31

About Boys Being Boys

I have so many good memories of coaching that I enjoy
thinking about, but the ones I am telling you here are among
the best.

Coach Joe B. Hall

Some of my experiences with the players make me smile every
time I think of them—for instance, the time I had to start
Freddie Cowan in place of Chuck Verderber. Chuck got hurt and
couldn't play in an important game we had coming up, so I had to
use Freddie Cowan in his place in the starting line-up. Freddie was
kind of a timid kid, but a good, sweet kid. He never said anything
much, no trash talk or anything like that. Whenever I or any of my
assistants would ask him to do something, he would always answer,
"Okeydokey." I wanted him to give me a more responsive answer.
I wanted him to explain or otherwise show me that he understood
what he had to do to replace Chuck Verderber. I wanted to inspire
a different reply from him.

After I'd sent the rest of the team out to get ready to start the
game, I got Freddie in the locker room and told him to sit down. I
pulled my chair up and sat directly in front of him. I said, "Freddie,
look at me. Look me in the eye. Do you realize your responsibility in
replacing Chuck Verderber?" No reply. "Do you know the physical
toughness you are going to have to find in yourself to replace him?"
No answer, but a slight nod.

Raising my voice and my blood pressure, I asked him, "Do
you know that Chuck is a real tough guy who can withstand the
intimidation of his opponents? He can block out shots with physical

effort and seal the defense. He is a real tough guy, a ball handler, and ball stealer. He will dive on the floor and mix it physically with his opponents! Are you going to give us that kind of effort, Freddie? Are you going to replace the assists that Chuck gives us? Are you going to toughen up and be the guy on the floor?" No answer. Just a blank stare.

Raising my voice even louder, I said, "Freddie, talk to me! Are you going to dominate? Are you ready to do that, Freddie?" He looked at me and said meekly, "Okeydokey, Coach." And I just wilted. Of course he wasn't ready. And he didn't do what I needed him to do in that game, but in two or three years, he overcame his retiring nature and made us a real good player. Freddie became a starter and a great contributor to our success.

I think it was Henry Fielding who said, "When boys are doing nothing, they are doing mischief." During the Christmas holidays, when the players were doing nothing, the regular dorm guards on night duty were given a few days off. I did not like leaving the players in the dorms all by themselves, so I hired an older retired man to stay awake in the dorm at night with them to see that all went well.

The second night he was there he called me near midnight, waking me up. He sounded frantic and scared. "Coach Hall! You gotta get down here right now." Standing there in my pajamas, not fully awake, I groaned, "Why? What is it?" He said, "There's been an awful fight upstairs. They got to fighting and making an awful racket, hollering and banging into the walls. There's a bunch of 'em up there. It's been awful. I rushed up the stairs to see what was going on, and, Coach Hall, I hate to tell you this, but I think they have killed Jim Duff." I said, stunned, "You think Jim Duff is dead?" He answered, "Yeah, I know it was Ronnie Lyons who done it too. They have got him lying on the floor in a pool of blood. He's not conscious and there's blood everywhere. When he said "blood," I immediately knew what had happened.

Ronnie Lyons and Walt McCombs, our trainer, loved going to the wrestling matches every week. They had become friends with a couple of the wrestlers. No doubt they had gotten some of that fake blood those wrestlers use and decided to play a trick on the old night watchman.

I told the old man, "You go back upstairs and you get right down in Jim Duff's ear and say Coach Hall is on the phone downstairs, and he wants to talk to you." The old man said, "Oh, no, Coach Hall, you don't understand. Jim Duff is knocked out cold and covered with blood. He ain't moving or breathing." I said, "No, sir, you do what I told you. Go back upstairs and tell that guy who is lying bloody on the floor that Coach Hall is on the phone and wants to talk to him right now."

Everything was quiet for a several minutes, then Jim picked up the phone and said very softly, "We're sorry, Coach Hall—we didn't think he would call you."

Another one of my all-time favorite stories happened right before a game began. That night I was starting with Steve Lochmueller instead of Kevin Grevey, who was one of my very best players and our highest scorer. Although I hated to, I had to bench Kevin for missing curfew. Missing curfew was a serious offense, and I would not stand for it. Lochmueller was a big kid, good-natured and fun to be around, but he probably ate himself out of being a good basketball player. His senior year he switched to football. It was a smart move because it gave him experience and knowledge of both sports. Because of his well-rounded total athletic college experience, he became the athletic director at Eastern Kentucky University.

While the boys were in the locker room getting ready for the game, my staff and I were in the adjacent room. The air duct between the rooms carried the players' voices. As usual we were not paying any attention to their chatter until we heard Lochmueller making an announcement to his buddies. Then in his loud booming voice he began doing an excellent imitation of our own very famous

UK radio broadcaster, who was known as the Voice of the Wildcats. Speaking with excitement in his "Cawood" voice, Lochmueller began:

> Good evening, ladies and gentlemen! This is Cawood Ledford coming to you from Memorial Coliseum as the University of Kentucky Wildcats take on the Auburn Tigers for supremacy in the Southeastern Conference. There is standing room only here in Memorial Coliseum. The fire marshal has turned his head while the largest crowd ever has assembled in this building. The atmosphere is so electric! You can feel it in the air as it raises the hair on the back of your neck.
>
> Now the teams are coming onto the floor! The starters for Kentucky tonight are Ronnie Lyons and Mike Flynn—guards; Bob Guyette—center; and forwards Jimmy Dan Conner and *the pride of Tell City, Indiana, six foot six Steeeeeeve Lochmueller!* We are ready to start! The official tosses the ball and Guyette gets the tip, tosses it to Mike Flynn, who calls time out! And—in comes Grevey!

Lochmueller was hilarious! My assistants and I just broke down laughing. He was saying you can bet Coach Hall won't start with Grevey but it won't be long before he puts him in. So he has me putting Grevey back in the game before there was any action. Of course, that's not the way it happened, but Lochmueller gave us all an unforgettable, delightful surprise that night.

32

Wildcat Lodge

After all those years of hearing about "Bear Bryant Hilton"
at Tuscaloosa and some other fine athletic dorms at other
schools, Kentucky finally got a place of its own in the Joe B.
Hall Wildcat Lodge.

Russell Rice

The idea of a separate living facility for the basketball team came
to me in 1977, after I spent a night in a dorm room waiting for
Kevin Grevey, who had missed curfew. I ended up having to stay the
entire night in Kevin's bed—he never came in until after I had left
in the morning. (But that's another story.) I learned that night how
difficult it was for the players to coexist with the regular students
who did not have curfews and who came in at all hours. The hall
was noisy all night long. Some kids were playing tennis in the hall
for a while. Also, some kid, I think it was Ronnie Lyons, would
quietly open the door a crack to peep in at regular intervals to see
if I was still there.

Friday nights in the dorms were party time, and that was
especially true on a pre-game night if we had a game on Saturday
night. It was impossible for the players to get a good night's sleep
with all the commotion going on in those dorms.

Another thing, the players were like rock stars. When a student
had visitors from his hometown, he wanted them to meet the ball
players and would think nothing of waking a player up to introduce
his friends to him. So many distractions were always present for
the players living among the regular students. Nothing bad, just
normal dorm life, but still, it made me think how good it would be
if I had a separate dorm for my team.

I had visited other colleges that had separate living spaces for their players. Alabama had a very fine dorm for its football team in Tuscaloosa, and so did LSU, Georgia, Kansas, Mississippi, and many others. I knew it would be a good thing if I could build such a structure on our campus for our players.

The first thing I did was go to Fran Curci, the football coach, and ask him if he wanted to join me in this project, which required us to raise money for an athletic dorm that would hold all the student athletes in all the sports. He did not want to participate. He wanted to give his players off-campus living in two or three houses. I did not like that idea at all. I did not want my players separated from each other. I wanted to build more unity. I asked Fran if he minded if I built a place just for my players. He said he did not mind at all.

Next I talked to Dr. Singletary who, as I have already explained, strongly favored the football program. He was not at all interested in basketball or in helping me with the program. He shrugged his shoulders as if he did not care for my idea and asked how much I thought such a dorm would cost. I said I figured it would cost close to $1 million to build a place large enough for all the players, and for a house family to oversee and manage the facility. It also had to be large enough to include rooms for a supervisor and a manager, plus dining and recreation areas.

If I wished to pursue my idea, Dr. Singletary said, rather firmly, I would have to raise all the money and—he emphasized—without using widespread radio, television, or newspapers ads. He did not offer any encouragement, or say he thought such a dorm would be great for the university. He did tell me that the university would provide the land on which to build it, and that it would have to be built according to the university's specifications. And, of course, he added, the university would own the deed to it at no cost. I left that afternoon with the impression that he did not think I could raise enough money for the construction.

After getting permission to go ahead, I turned to my good friends Andy Palmer and Don and Dudley Webb, who were the shakers and movers in Kentucky. They were always either leading or involved in important projects that promoted the Commonwealth's growth. They were also lawyers and huge supporters of the UK Wildcats. The four of us created the Wildcat Foundation, Inc., and in less than a month we raised enough money to build the dorm. I am sure Dr. Singletary was surprised.

Everyone we contacted thought the dorm was a grand idea and was happy to donate what amount he or she could. We took in small gifts and large ones. When those $25,000 checks started coming in, we decided to name rooms after those donors. Wonderful too were the builders, electricians, plumbers, and painters who donated their services and materials.

While I was in Louisville one weekend, where we were to play Notre Dame, I learned that Brown Badgett Sr., a wealthy coal man from western Kentucky and a great fan of Kentucky basketball, was staying at our hotel. I wanted to meet him and was told he was in the hotel bar having a drink. I introduced myself, sat down with him, and told him I wanted to build a dorm for the basketball players and why it was necessary to do so. He asked, "Well, what do you want from me?" I explained that we were naming rooms for anyone who contributed $25,000. A half of a real basketball and a small bronze plaque with the donor's name would be mounted onto a board and placed near the door of each room. He said, "Give me two rooms." I said, "What?" He said, "I'll take two rooms!"

After we realized we shared a great love for fishing, he and I became great friends. I went with him on his private jet on at least eight fishing trips abroad through the years. We fished in Brazil, Africa, Canada, New Mexico, and Venezuela, just to name a few places. We always had a great time together. C. M. Newton and some others would often go with us.

There were many others in the coal industry and in other industries that helped us. We were blessed with generous donors. Plus, we had tremendous help from a local men's group called the Alley Cats. I want to tell you about them.

In the 1960s, a group of business and professional men, about thirty or thirty-five of them, met at the YMCA on High Street in Lexington every Wednesday night at 5:30. (And they still do.) They played basketball, then showered, had dinner, and listened to a speaker. Usually the speaker's topic would be in athletics, education, or politics. These men were all great Wildcat fans.

One night after discussing how basketball fans far outnumbered the available seats in Memorial Coliseum, one of the men, Jim Dunden, I think it was, revealed that if he wanted to see a game and didn't have tickets, he would go to the alley behind Memorial Coliseum to try to buy a ticket from someone or get in through the back door somehow to see if he could buy one inside. He exclaimed, "It's getting so now, to see a Kentucky game, we all have to become alley cats!" Hence, this group of men named themselves the Alley Cats.

It was a plain fact that the Coliseum was far too small for the crowds we were having. People were lining the walls, despite the fire marshal's rules. We needed a new and much larger stadium. This was in the mid- to late 1960s when two members of the men's group, Roy Holsclaw, a dentist, and Elbert Ray, an architect, decided to do a feasibility study for a basketball stadium. They were thinking too it could be named after Coach Rupp, who would be made to retire when he reached seventy.

When the football coach learned what they were doing, he asked if they would also do a feasibility study on a football stadium. They agreed. After they completed their work, about two years later, they sent copies of their studies to the university and to the governor's office.

During the last week in January 1972, after the governor had read both feasibility studies, he invited Roy and Elbert and other members of the group to come to a meeting in Frankfort. Present at that meeting also was Dr. Singletary, Larry Forgy, and some other vice presidents from the university. Fred Wachs, the owner of both Lexington newspapers—the *Herald* and the *Leader*—was also there.

Governor Louie Nunn welcomed everyone and asked, "What can I do for you, gentlemen?" Dr. Singletary stood up and said, "Governor, we want you to build a new football stadium." And he sat down. There was only silence for about fifteen or twenty seconds. Roy said that he, Elbert, and the others in the group were shocked that Dr. Singletary did not mention the basketball stadium, but no one said anything.

Governor Nunn, who must have also been surprised, asked, "Is that all you want, Dr. Singletary?" And Dr. Singletary replied, "Yes, Governor Nunn, we ask for just half a loaf this time." Then Governor Nunn turned to Fred Wachs and asked, "Mr. Wachs, if we build a football stadium, will your newspapers support us?" He answered, "Governor, we will not support it if you build it out on that property the university owns called Cold Stream Farm, on the north side of Lexington, near the interstate. But if you build it on the campus, where the students can easily get to it, we will support it."

The governor ended the meeting and walked to where Roy and the other Alley Cats were standing and said, "I read your feasibility reports you sent me. You recommend we build both stadiums. Are you going to oppose my building this football stadium?" They told the governor no, they were not opposed to it, but that they wanted both stadiums and were disappointed that Dr. Singletary did not ask for a basketball arena too.

That's when Governor Nunn nodded and said, "Yes, I'd like to build the football and the basketball stadium, side by side, right there on the campus, where there are lights, parking, and convenient walking distances for students. That's where they ought to be! I'd name it the *Nunn Complex!*"

And he was right, that's where both stadiums should be. Financially, that location would have benefited the university and the athletic programs. It just made sense to build it there.

Roy's group told the governor that they would continue to pursue their goal to build a new basketball stadium. And that's what they did. They gathered their feasibility study and ideas they had about how and where it could be built and presented it all in a meeting with the mayor of Lexington and the city government officials, who were all pleased with the idea. Thus, we have Rupp Arena!

In the fall of 1977, we started construction of the Wildcat Lodge on the property the university had designated, which was across the street from Memorial Coliseum and near the Student Union and classrooms. With our own money, we bought an adjacent lot and house owned by an elderly woman. That lot gave us a good bit more space. We found another house nearby for her to move into, and she was pleased with the move.

We hired Barbara Riche, a twenty-four-year-old, talented, hard-working, pleasant Lexington interior decorator. The first thing I told her was I wanted this dorm to look like a ski lodge, not a post office, bank, or office building. I wanted it to be built and furnished with materials from Kentucky only. I wanted it to be masculine in taste, colors, and furnishings, and the furniture had to be large, comfortable, and durable. "Just think of a ski lodge, Barbara." And I told her it all had to have the approval of the NCAA. I did not want us to do anything to get kicked out of that organization.

At her own expense, Barbara started out by traveling to different colleges to see their athletes' dorms, and she paid close attention to the NCAA requirements. Cliff Hagan, our athletic director, and I stayed in close contact with the NCCA home office, which was located in Kansas at that time. I am stressing the fact that everything we did from the very beginning had been first approved by the NCAA.

Before the lodge was under construction, Barbara took all her floor plans, sketches, and boards of what we planned to do and made a presentation to the NCAA officers. No one could have been more conscientious than she about doing "everything by the NCAA book!" The NCAA officers told Barbara they were very pleased with what she was doing and to go ahead with her plans.

She designed the interior so that each of the thirteen players had a small bedroom, maybe twelve by twelve, with a twin bed that was either eight or nine feet long but remained only three feet wide. We had the beds made of Kentucky wood and designed so that our players would find them comfortable. The regular-sized twin beds they had been sleeping on in no way accommodated young men who were all over six feet tall or even near seven feet, like Sam Bowie. With few exceptions, each boy weighed two hundred pounds or more.

Each room had a study area because we emphasized the importance of academics. The ceilings were high, of course, and every room had a small bathroom with a tall shower and a raised toilet. The vanity tops were about forty-eight inches. Everything was made to accommodate the height and weight of the players, and they appreciated those accommodations very much.

Barbara designed a large entry or living room with comfortable chairs, a television, and stairs to the upper story. A dining area was downstairs. The boys had breakfast there every morning before they left for class. Memorial Coliseum was just a few steps away, and their classrooms were nearby. It was an ideal location.

All that Cliff Hagan, my fundraisers, Barbara, and I did had been approved by the UK athletic department and by the NCAA. Remember that fact! The lodge was complete by Christmas 1977. After all the construction workers took their equipment and left for good, some of the players and I cleaned up the yard around the lodge, as we had been doing every afternoon after the construction crews left for the day. Then Barbara, together with some other ladies who volunteered to help her that Sunday, cleaned the inside of the lodge using their own supplies. The team moved in the next day, the Monday after Christmas 1977.

Before we gave the lodge to the university, we needed to put the sign on it. The Alley Cats, according to Roy Holsclaw, thought that because it had been my idea to build the place and I had worked so hard on the project with them, it should be named after me. The Alley Cats had helped raise much of the money to build it and were able to pay for the construction and furnishing in full for it—and still had money left over—so they figured they had the right to name the lodge and without conferring first with the university. Roy said they unanimously wanted to name it after me. I was flattered, of course.

Roy also said that he and a couple of others had talked to guys at the campus physical plant about making the sign. This plant made aluminum signs, among other objects, for the university. Roy paid these workers to make us a nice large sign reading "Joe B. Hall Wildcat Lodge," and the workers placed that sign firmly in front of the lodge one afternoon after the boys had moved in. It all looked great. I felt so good about it. We all did. We were all happy.

A few days later, I was having dinner in the Duck Club room at the Hyatt Regency with Jerry Tarkanian, coach of the University of Las Vegas, the team that we were to play the next night. A couple of angry-looking friends came into the dining room and told me that the university workers had just removed my name from their sign, leaving only Wildcat Lodge. They wanted to know why the university thought it had the right to do that when the university had not helped pay for the lodge or the sign. They said, "We paid the university workmen to make our sign! It is our sign." Thus, they did not see why they did not have the right to name the building. Why would the university even have to be involved?

According to Roy, he and a couple of others called Andy Palmer, a friend and strong supporter living in Frankfort. Andy was an attorney working for the state and the governor. He didn't live in Lexington, so he was not a member of the original group of Alley Cats, but he supported their cause. He was also a good friend of Julian Carroll, the governor, and he explained to the governor the trouble we were having with the sign. And that very same day, the workmen were back, replacing my name on the sign.

Roy said the head workman told him that he had been instructed to correct the sign and place it in front of the lodge that very day. The employee, chuckling, said the governor's office had phoned the president's office that morning saying, "Dr. Singletary, the governor thinks you should put Joe Hall's name back on that sign ASAP."

Larry Ivy, one of the UK administrators, explained to Roy and the others that the university had a special committee whose job it was to name buildings on campus, and that the Alley Cats had not gone through the proper channels before placing the sign. At any rate, it all ended well.

After we had paid all of our bills, we still had $125,000 left. We gave all that money to the university so that they could put great lights on the dorm, the parking lot, the tennis courts, outside basketball courts, and the baseball field, which we also built. We really lit the grounds up so the students could enjoy playing as late as they wished.

Just before the lodge was completed, Dr. Jackson, who had long served as the Wildcats' physician, came to me asking if he and Mrs. Jackson could move into the lodge and be "house parents" for the boys. I was surprised that Mrs. Jackson would give up her lovely home to live in the limited space we could provide. But Dr. Jackson said no, they wanted to live in the lodge. That would mean we would be the only men's dormitory with a live-in doctor and nurse. With the Good Samaritan Hospital ER right across the street, we could boast to the parents of our recruits how well prepared we were to take care of their sons if they were injured or became ill. What a comfort it was for parents to know that we would take good care of their son.

I remember Tom Parker's parents telling me how distressed they were with the college their other son was attending. He had gotten very ill with the flu, and no one came to look after him or even notify his parents that he was seriously ill. So having Dr. Jackson and his wife was a real plus for our lodge.

A few weeks after the Jacksons had settled in the little apartment we created for them, Dr. Jackson came to me again. He quietly asked me if the donor's name on the plaque near his door could be removed. The name, he said, upset his wife Marie. He explained that the name on the engraved plaque was that of his first wife, whom he had divorced to marry Marie. I did not know the $25,000 donor or anything about his first marriage. I told him I understood and would have the name changed immediately. So we named the suite of rooms after Dr. Jackson and his second wife, who had donated their services to us.

After we had won the title in 1978 and had enjoyed living in the lodge for a little over a year, some other coaches began to grumble about us. They were saying that because Kentucky had this "plush" house, they could more easily recruit and get better players. Enough of them complained that the NCAA came down hard on us in the summer of 1979, reversing things they had approved earlier.

The NCAA officer told the UK athletic director and me to get rid of all our blue and white phones and replace them with black ones. He told us to put padlocks on all the private bathroom doors and ordered us to use two rooms on each floor to build common bathrooms and showers. The long beds the players could sleep so comfortably in had to be sold and replaced with the standard twin-size beds, seventy-two inches long.

The rooms were small, not built to accommodate two boys, yet the NCAA had us put two beds, two desks, two chairs, and two boys in each room. Then the NCAA required us to have a few nonatheletes—regular students—live in the lodge. We could not treat the basketball players in such a special way without including regular students. The NCAA stopped the lodge from serving breakfast except during holidays when the cafeteria was closed. Also, they had us remove the steps to the upstairs that were in our large entry room and build stairs on the sides of the building. To go to his room from the entry room, a player would have to go outside, walk around to the side of the building, and go through a side door that led to a stairway to the top floors.

Our beautiful fireplaces made of coal from different places in Kentucky were boarded up. A wall was constructed to separate the building into two sections. Part of the space was to be used for living quarters, and the other part stayed closed, opened only for special events. We had a pool table and a ping-pong table. We were told to get rid of one. The big study area upstairs was closed off completely.

It was all very upsetting. Many of our boosters and fans wanted us to file a lawsuit against the NCAA because they had approved our plans just two years earlier. We chose to comply instead. But yes, you can bet it was distressing! Especially when we knew that other colleges were not being required to make similar changes.

33

NCAA Championship, 1978

One man can be a crucial ingredient on a team, but one man cannot make a team.

Kareem Abdul-Jabbar

In 1978, Rick Robey, Jack Givens, Mike Phillips, and James Lee were seniors, serious and mature. They were determined to win a NCAA championship before they graduated. As freshmen, they lost the 1975 championship against UCLA. That tournament was held in San Diego, where none of the players had been before and were excited about going. Once they got to California, they did as much sightseeing as possible. I am retelling this so you will know that although they were serious about winning the game, they were also distracted and relaxed. That frame of mind is not good to have before an important battle.

This time in 1978, they made up their minds at the start of the season they were going to win Kentucky's fifth national title, and they never wavered from their goal. They had no interest in sightseeing in St. Louis, where the tournament was to be held. On the other hand, it was interesting for me to go back to St. Louis, where I had gone a few years earlier to accept a job offer after my life at UK had become unbearable because of Coach Rupp's treatment.

In the semi-finals of the NCAA tournament, after Duke beat Notre Dame, the Duke team celebrated loudly and joyfully. We could hear them laughing and hollering in the locker room after the game as they threw each other into the shower. They even threw in their fully dressed coach Bill Foster. While Duke celebrated loudly, my boys got dressed quietly. They had already shifted their thoughts to the final game. Even newspaper reporters commented on how serious and "grim-faced" Kentucky players were.

After they got dressed, I asked them if they would like to go to some nice restaurant rather than eat at the hotel where we were staying, and then to a movie to relax. No one answered. Then Robey said, "Coach, didn't you say you taped that Duke game? Could we stay in our rooms and order room service and watch that film?" And so that's what we did.

The boys on that team bonded into strong and lasting friendships. Nothing is more rewarding in coaching than to see that kind of bonding take place. Every one of those guys performed well in every game. Each player worked smoothly with the others. They functioned like nimble fingers on one hand. In that final game against Duke, every member of our team played an important role.

In fact, different players throughout all the games we played that year came to the front to star. When we played Florida State, the first game in the NCAA tournaments, and were behind seven points at half-time, I put the subs in and they played great. After the starters saw what the subs were doing, they worked harder. We won that game!

Another time when we played Miami of Ohio, Mike Phillips was the star. When we played Michigan State, which had probably the best player in the country—Magic Johnson—our Kyle Macy hit eight straight free throws down the stretch. We set him up with screens as our scoring weapon in the second half. What an exciting game that was!

Then, in the game against Arkansas during the semi-finals, every player contributed. I never forgot how hurtful it was when I was a young sub for Coach Rupp. He never let us play, not even when we were way ahead. I vowed back then that if I ever coached, I would let every sub play.

A perfect example of the kind of teamwork every coach loves to see occurred in the finals when the zone defense that Duke played opened up for Jack Givens. My kids felt no selfishness and gave Jack the ball every time he was open. They knew he could put the ball in the basket, and they let him. Duke was never able to stop him. Jack was amazing that night. He scored forty-one points because the other players put him in the right position to do so. That's teamwork!

Even Duke coach Bill Foster said Jack was phenomenal: "I don't think anybody scored that many points on us all year. . . . He just had a fantastic game. He scored from everywhere" ("Givens' Greatest Game Powers Wildcats to Fifth NCAA Crown in Two Decades," *Lexington Leader*, March 28, 1978).

Jack's mother was watching from her front-row seat. He had said earlier that night that he wanted to make his mother proud of him, and he surely did. Mrs. Givens was overwhelmed with pride. We were all proud of Jack.

Kyle Macy did a great job too. I had tried to recruit him in Indiana and Truman Claytor in Ohio at the same time. I really wanted both guards. They were ideally suited to work together. Truman accepted my last scholarship, but Kyle ended up registering at Purdue. After he had attended a year at Purdue, his dad called me saying his son wanted to transfer to UK and would I help. I explained that I could not be a part of a transfer, that he had to contact Purdue's athletic director and have him make the transfer with our athletic director. I was happy to learn that he wanted to join us. Truman made the perfect off guard with Kyle.

Kyle was an outstanding player, and he fitted our style of playing perfectly. He was a smart point guard, an excellent shooter, and he set free-throw shooting records. He remained calm under pressure. He was just a good all-round, smart, heady basketball player, with size and ball-handling ability. Kyle Macy was the whole package!

He came to us in the summer, moved in with the Wildcats, and got a summer job. Of course he had to sit out a year, but during that year he studied and worked out with the players daily. He had them teach him the offense. He studied tapes of games, and by the first day of practice in the fall of his eligibility year he understood our complete offense and could run all of our drills. He was that heady and competitive. He wanted to play. After Larry Johnson graduated in 1977, Kyle was the perfect guy to replace him. It was his leadership, too, that carried us through the rough season and to the final game.

To show you just how important his leadership role was, here's Al McGuire's unflattering metaphor describing my team: "To stop a snake, you have to cut his head off. To beat Kentucky, you have to cut Kyle Macy out."

Kyle was not only a great scorer and a complete teammate, he was the best feeder of the low post we ever had. Robey and Phillips absolutely loved him. He would get the ball to them on the inside. When they called on Macy to get the ball to them in our game against Michigan State in the NCAA Mideast Regionals in 1978, he did so magnificently. Michigan State had a guard so great they nicknamed him Magic! Yes, that's Earvin Johnson. What Michigan State didn't know is we had our own magic—Kyle Macy hit eight free throws down the stretch in the last crucial minutes.

Rick Robey had a fine game too. He was the only other player who scored in double digits, with twenty points. I was proud of my reserves as well. They were Dwane Casey, James Lee, Jay Shidler, LaVon Williams, Fred Cowan, Scott Courts, and Chuck Aleksinas. When you win a national championship, the last guy on the bench makes a solid contribution with his attitude. And if he is called on, he does his best. That's what's so good about competition. When you set your mind to win, you don't play to help yourself. You play to help your teammates. That Duke game was a perfect example of players getting the ball to the guy who was in the best spot to score. And I am sure a lot of them would have liked to take some shots themselves, but the play of the night was Jack getting those little soft jumpers. He was so good at that. He was master at the little floater in the fifteen-foot area.

The proof of that team's bonding is evident in their annual

reunions. Once a year since 1978 they get together in Lexington. Until recently, now that my health is not good, I enjoyed attending those reunions. Not all of the teams bonded like that one, but I know that the Fabulous Five did and also Rupp's Runts. Although they lost their finals, the Runts continue to communicate with each other and have annual get-togethers.

During that summer of '78 after we won the championship, we were invited by the Japanese Basketball Federation to play the Japanese national team in eight different cities. They would pay all of our expenses. All we had to do was show up and play. The guys were excited about going to Asia and thought the trip just added more icing to their cake!

The day of our arrival in Tokyo for the final game, three impressive-looking gentlemen, all representatives of the Tiger Shoe Company, came to my hotel room with boxes and boxes of all kinds of electronic gifts. They spread them all out on the floor to show me. Then the leader of the group offered to give me these gifts if I would have our players wear their Tiger shoes in the game that they were to play in Tokyo.

I told him no for several reasons. One reason was that we were contracted to Converse, and Converse furnished our shoes. Another reason was I didn't want my players to be wearing new shoes in a game for the first time. I'd have the boys always break in new shoes gradually, wearing them at first for only part of the time in a few practices. The Tiger reps nodded, showing they understood and accepted my reasons. They packed their presents, thanked me, and went on their way.

Later that evening at the game, I was on the floor watching the players warming up when I looked under the team bench and saw a pair of Converse shoes. I asked Mr. Keightley, our equipment manager, "Bill, what's these shoes doing under the bench?" He answered, "Oh, Jack is warming up in Tiger shoes. He'll change to his Converse for the game." I told him that I had turned the Tiger

Company down. He said, "Yeah, we know. But they got to Jack."
I laughed, wondering what the Tiger reps had given Jack. I didn't
see anything and I didn't ask. Jack had finished his eligibility and
graduated. It was okay.

34

That Georgetown Game, 1984

I've missed more than 9,000 shots in my career. I've lost almost 300 games. 26 times I've been trusted to take the game winning shot and missed. I've failed over and over and over again in my life. And that's why I succeed.

Michael Jordan

Another game I want to talk about is the one we played with Georgetown in the 1984 NCAA semi-finals. This team dominated us physically, but we were ahead at half-time and looking great.

We came out of the locker room at the second half feeling good. We had played as good a game as we could play up to that point. Then all of sudden it was as if the lights went out—in our heads. We hit only three of thirty-three attempts in the second half. It was horrifying! We shot 9 percent. Never in my career, from high school on up, did I ever witness a team that could not make a layup. It was something unreal! I don't know what happened to my boys. That was a nightmare for me. It would be for any coach to watch his players miss shot after shot after shot. I have never even looked at the film. I don't want to see it.

In a radio interview after the game, I said that there must have been some kind of mystical force created by the Georgetown physics department that pulled the ball away from the basket whenever we shot. James Blackmon, one of our best shooters, went in for a wide-open layup, and the ball circled the rim and dropped out. Dropped out! There had to have been some kind of magical vibration to move the ball away from the basket *every* time one of my boys took a shot. We were a team that would shoot 50 percent or better, and that night we shot 9 percent—three of our thirty-three attempts. You cannot imagine how painful it was to sit there and watch players as good as Sam Bowie and Melvin Turpin miss shots that they normally made. I could not understand it. The boys couldn't understand it either.

Losing that game to Georgetown kept me from retiring that year as I had planned. I did not want to leave the coach who followed with that kind of situation. Plus, we were losing so many starters and key players. I would have been ashamed to leave the program in that kind of shape. So I stayed through 1984–1985 to get in a good recruiting year and leave my successor with better conditions.

That 1984–1985 year those boys came together and did really well. And 1984–1985 turned out to be a real good year. Those kids worked together so well. They battled all the adversity that had surrounded them. And then in the end they beat two excellent teams—UNLV and Washington—in the playoff games and made it to the regionals to play St. John's.

We played St. John's in Denver, which gave me a chance to introduce my team at Regis College, where I had coached for six years. I enjoyed returning there. I took the team to the small gym at Regis to practice. It was so good to see that many of the teachers and the Jesuit priests I knew were still there, and they welcomed me with open arms. That visit was a highlight for me. Instead of wearing my usual blue suit, I wore a brown one. I had never worn brown to any of the games before because Coach Rupp always wore brown.

Just when everything was going well and we had an early lead of 20–13, a tragic accident occurred. St. John's player Chris Mullins accidentally poked his finger into the eye of my star player, Kenny Walker. Chris apologized to Kenny immediately. We were convinced it was an accident, but still it took its toll. For much of that first half, Kenny sat on the bench pressing an ice pack to his swollen eye. After a while he wanted to get back in the game.

Even though depth perception is changed when you try to shoot with one eye, Kenny still scored twenty-three points in that game. Although we lost to St. John's 86–70, I thought that the season had been rewarding and the team had worked through problems they had earlier. I was proud of them. That was the night I announced my retirement.

I never wanted to be an old coach. I had seen too many of them. Besides that, I knew there were other jobs that I could do. So when I decided to announce my retirement, I announced I was retiring from full-time coaching only. Also, it seemed fitting that I end my college coaching career there at Regis, in Denver, Colorado, where it began.

35

Life After Coaching

Do not complain about growing old. It is a privilege denied to many.

Mark Twain

For those first few months after I retired from coaching in April 1985, I did nothing but loaf around and fish. Fishing always relaxes me. Then, when the first hint of fall appeared in the air, I decided to go back to work. Earl Wilson, the chairman of the board at Central Bank, had asked me while I was still coaching if after I retired I would come work for the bank. I told him then that I would like that and would be back in touch at some later date.

So that fall I called him, saying I was ready to work, if he still needed me. I was made senior vice president of correspondent management, and my role was dealing with other banks. It required some traveling, which I have always enjoyed. I liked my bank job and stayed for over twelve years. In the course of that job, I met so many new people with whom I am friends to this day.

On weekends, I worked for ABC for about five years, doing some color-commentary broadcasting for several play-by-play celebrities. I worked with Al Michaels, Keith Jackson, Gary Bender, and Dick Vitale. I'd often leave on Friday night and return home Sunday. I traveled all over the country and did about ten games a year for ABC. I enjoyed that job as well. It was great visiting with other coaches whom I had known throughout the years and meeting the new younger ones.

One time while I was in California calling a game for UCLA, I asked about Coach Wooden and was told he was at that very moment out on the track doing his daily several-mile walk. I caught up with him on the track and while we walked we talked about our experiences. It was a very good visit. I was comfortable enough with him that afternoon to bring up the reason I thought my Wildcats lost that NCAA championship in 1975 to his Bruins. I told him how unfair it was for him to announce before the game that he was going to retire. "Coach, I know you planned to win that championship, using your announcement to get everyone excited." He didn't say anything, just tucked his head down and chuckled. We had a few laughs about other old times. Coach Wooden lived to be ninety-nine years old. His daily walks surely must have contributed to his longevity. He was a good man. I liked him.

Our paths crossed several times after we both were retired. One time when Texas Roadhouse sponsored a basketball weekend in Cabo San Lucas, Mexico, three other retired NCAA championship coaches and I were invited. John Wooden from UCLA, Denny Crum from the University of Louisville, Nolan Richardson from the University of Arkansas, and I were supposedly to coach the teams Texas Roadhouse had lined up among their managers and play against one another. It was a job that made us laugh and kid around with each other a lot. We all had a good time that weekend in that beautiful location.

In 1988, Terry McBrayer and I went fishing at Lake of the Woods in northwestern Ontario, Canada. We stayed at Ash Rapids Camp fishing for smallmouth bass. One night, I began hemorrhaging from my bowels. The operators of the camp called a helicopter and flew me to Kenora, where I was taken to a small hospital, put on a steel gurney, and left in a hallway, waiting for the one doctor, who was in surgery. After I had waited an hour or more, a large Native American nurse entered and addressed the patient lineup: "Bleeders first; broken bones second; fish hooks last." There were six little boys with fish hooks stuck in various places on their bodies.

After I was taken into the surgery area, the doctor showed me on a video screen the cancer in my colon. He explained that the huge blob of stuff I was seeing on the screen was definitely malignant and needed to be cut out as soon as possible. I told him I wanted to go back home for the surgery, and he agreed.

After I left the hospital with my diagnosis that late morning, I called home and I asked my friend Ed Neibert, a vascular surgeon, if he had removed any cancers from a colon. He said it was simple to do, and he would take care of me. Terry and I went back to our fishing, and we fished until dark. The next day, my friend Brown Badgett, who had been fishing at his camp in Fort Francis, Canada, flew us home in his private plane. Dr. Neibert removed the cancer and three feet of my colon, and I have never had any trouble since.

During the period I was with the bank and ABC, I did broadcasts for UK home games on the local television station, and I also did games all over the country for Westwood One Radio. Then one day I got two very interesting coaching offers from two big companies in Japan: Sekisui, which made chemicals, and Dawia, a producer of fishing equipment. Each wanted to hire me to coach their women's pro basketball teams. Their offers were too good to ignore, and I knew my wife loved visiting such foreign places. So I quit my jobs with the bank, television, and radio stations, and we went to Kyoto, Japan.

Katharine made many of my trips abroad with me, and she always went to the clinics. She loved shopping in foreign countries and especially in Japan and in Korea, where she had a real feast. She bought all kinds of fans, screens, silverware, and hand-painted dishes, especially these huge beautifully painted platters. Not only did she buy things for herself, she chose gifts for the children, family members, and friends. I think the only thing I bought for myself on that trip was a pair of my prescription glasses for $25.

Dawia was the first company to call me. The caller explained what they wanted me to do for two full months, where I would live, and where the practices would be held. When I asked him how I was to get to and from the gym, he hesitated a long time—too long—and then asked, "Do you ride bicycle?" I declined his offer and instead signed a contract with Sekisui, which provided a driver for me. We left the United States for Japan on the last day of September 1996. I coached that women's pro team for two months—all of October and November. Because of Japanese customs, I sometimes had trouble motivating the women players to practice some moves. I remember being particularly frustrated one day while I was demonstrating how to set a trap in a pressing defense. I told them they had to be fearless. I said for them to think of themselves as bears jumping out from behind a tree and growling fiercely. I demonstrated by growling loudly. For reasons unknown to me, they thought I was funny and broke out giggling—not growling. However, they were good ball handlers and their shooting was excellent. They made over 80 percent of their free throws. We won 80 percent of our games.

Katharine returned home after a week, and later my son Steve came over and stayed with me the last two weeks I was there. We returned home early in December, just a few days after attending—and I might add enjoying—the big birthday dinner party the company and the team had for me on November 30 when I turned sixty-eight.

After I returned home to Lexington, I went back to work for Westwood One Sports radio. I had finished calling a game in Iowa for them that weekend and was at the airport walking fast to the gate where I could board my plane home when I felt a sudden pain under my left shoulder. It was the kind of pain that reminds one of his mortality. When I stopped to rest, the pain would go away. Then when I resumed walking, it started again.

As soon as I got home, I went to see Dr. Shine, my family doctor, who hooked me up to a treadmill. Within two minutes, he stopped the machine and said, "You are coming with me." He drove straight to the hospital, where the next morning I had bypass surgery. One of my main arteries was 98 percent blocked. Dr. Bob Sallee, the surgeon, called it "the widow maker." Unfortunately, I soon developed a high fever caused by a yeast infection in the incision.

This infection had eaten into my sternum, and I was dangerously ill. Dr. Sallee reopened the incision and removed all the dead tissue and cleaned the area. He saved my life and I am indebted to him.

The incision healed and I never have had any problems with it. But since then, I have developed diabetes, atrial fibrillation, and arthritis. Dr. Gary Grisby has placed five stints in my arteries and a pacemaker in my chest. He keeps a regular check on me, for which I am grateful. Despite all of these conditions and aches and pains, I am thankful for my life and I believe every day is a great day.

After that series of health issues, I finally retired. Then one morning I was sitting in Wheeler's Drug Store with Dick Robinson, an old friend. We had just finished lunch, and I was doing an interview on a radio program called the *Sonny and Wimp Show*. Sonny Smith from Auburn and Wimp Sanderson from Alabama were two popular basketball coaches who had a call-in talk show. I was a frequent guest on their program and always enjoyed talking with them. As I was answering a question, Dick scribbled something on a paper napkin and pushed it over in front of me. I read, "Joe B. and Denny Show!" Wow! As soon as the interview ended, I looked at Dick in amazement and said, "What a wonderful idea! Let's call Jim Host to see what he thinks!"

Jim Host was the mastermind behind all kinds of communication projects in Kentucky. He had developed many successful television and radio programs and was involved in many other areas of communication. And everything he did was great! I knew if he were involved, the program would succeed. Well, Jim was excited about our idea and as eager to pursue the project as Dick and I were. He told us, "You're dang right it'll go, and I want to be a part of it." Then I said, "Okay, let's call Denny now and get him on board."

As many of you know, Denny Crum and I were rivals while he coached the University of Louisville basketball team and I the Wildcats at the University of Kentucky. As you know, too, in-state rivals are the fiercest kind. On the floor Denny and I were real rivals, but off the floor we were good friends. He is a master hunter and fisherman, and we have had some memorable times hunting and fishing together in many places, including Canada and Alaska. I was happy when he was as excited about the radio program as I was. He said, "I'm in!"

As it turned out, Jim Host couldn't be a part of our project because the governor called about the same time needing Jim to do some important work for him. Of course, when the governor needs you to do something for the state, you do it.

I was seventy-five years old at the time and happily starting out on another new exciting career. Having that kind of job made me so happy to wake up in the mornings, get out of my pajamas, and get dressed to go "to work!"—except it was not work. It was fun! It was the best job I ever had. I loved working with Denny, visiting with other coaches, and talking to basketball fans from all over the state and outside of it too. Occasionally we talked with some of our own players.

After my friend Dick Robinson, our manager, passed away, Jim Lankster took his place. Jim and I have been friends for many years. He had been one of my assistant coaches at UK. He has a gift for organizing, communicating, and managing people and schedules. And he is a great chef!

One of our favorite listeners was a man we called "Ronnie on the bucket." The first time he called us, he said, "My name is Ronnie. I love your show. I listen every day. And I love those Wildcats." I asked him what was all that noise I was hearing in the background: "Where are you, Ronnie? What are you doing?" He answered, "I am out here in the woods with my dogs running some rabbits, and I am sitting on a bucket." When Dave Jennings heard that, he searched and found a record of an old song titled "My Bucket's Got a Hole in It and I Got Nobody to Buy My Beer." Every time after that when Ronnie called, Dave would play the first few lines of that song.

After such introductions to his calls, he'd get serious and start talking about how the Cats would do in their upcoming game. He followed the games carefully. A few months ago, Ronnie passed away, and a couple of men and I went to his funeral in Benton, Kentucky.

Since I was a child, I have always enjoyed meeting new people, and I know having that characteristic helped me with my recruiting. The radio program gave me the opportunity to talk to so many people I would otherwise never have known. Even more important, it brought Denny and me closer now we were not able to hunt and fish as we once did.

I loved doing that call-in program and was sad when it came to an end after ten years. The managers of the station wanted to change the format. We would no longer be a live call-in show, and our program wouldn't work well any other way. Denny and I could not go along with that change, and so we sadly bowed out. I wish we were still doing it today.

As I look back across the years, I know I was so fortunate to get to be the head of a program that had a great following and the respect of everyone who loved basketball. I am grateful for the fans and the boosters who helped me in so many ways. Oftentimes, they provided their private airplanes for us to go scout and recruit, and they found summer jobs for my players. Whatever project I wanted to do or whatever I needed, they were always there to help me. As it is often said today, it takes a village to raise children. Well, it takes a village to produce a great basketball program and team as well.

I was blessed to have assistant coaches who were loyal and hardworking; without them, no coach could be a success. No matter how smart you are as a coach, if you don't have good people in your organization you will not be successful. You must have a staff of secretaries, managers, equipment people, and so on who are all good, and who work as a team for a single goal. You need to have unselfish players who see the big picture and put teamwork above themselves. I had all of those factors in my program. I had the best group of assistants any coach could possible have. Most of my assistants went on to become college-level coaches themselves. Many of my players went on to have successful careers in the pros. Others went on to have careers in law, medicine, business, and in many other areas. I am so proud of every single one of my boys.

Although many of our players were not native Kentuckians, they chose to live and work and raise their families here. It makes me proud to see the genuine fellowship among them all. They continue to keep in contact with each other, and a few teams have annual reunions. And they still include me.

I don't get out now as much as I once did, but I have family and good friends who visit and take me to ball games, to local events, and also to lunch a couple of times a week at the nearby cafe at the Immanuel Baptist Church. Life is good!

36

Farewell

Death leaves a heartache no one can heal, love leaves a
memory no one can steal.

Irish headstone

As I look back across the years, it seems as if when something
bad happened to me, such as I didn't get the raise that I had
hoped for or I got the feeling that I was not making advances, I
was quick to move on to another situation or learn to adapt to the
situation I had.

When I think back, I see now that whenever Coach Rupp did
something that disappointed me, something good always followed.
For example, shortly before he was forced to retire, he refused to
admit during a televised interview that he had in a previous televised
interview promised to name me his successor. His denial came as
a surprise to me and many others who had heard him say that he
would. One such person was the television station manager, who
was present when Coach Rupp said he would name me. The station
manager had recorded and saved the tape of that program. After
Coach Rupp's denial, that recording was found in the station's file
stacks. The station manager replayed that first tape on his evening
broadcast a day or so after Coach Rupp's denial, proving that Coach
Rupp was not telling the truth. I did not know that tape recording
had ever been made, much less saved.

Another example occurred after I developed heart trouble and
had to give up coaching. That event led me to broadcasting which,
in turn, led me to a much better, more enjoyable life. So you see,
something bad has most often, in my life, at least, been followed by
something good. And so it had been until 2007.

Katharine had never been one to complain or to take "sick days." She was always busy taking care of us, her family, and my basketball players if they weren't well. She had a soft spot in her heart for those boys who lived far away from their homes and families, and she nursed them in the same manner she nursed us. If she did not feel well, she worked right on through her daily routines, tending to my needs and our children's and grandchildren's.

In the summer of 2006, I noticed that she had lost some weight and said something to her about it. She told me she had needed to lose a few pounds and felt better thinner. Then, in late February, she came down with what I thought might have been pneumonia, and I took her to Dr. James Borders, our highly respected family doctor. He hospitalized her immediately. I was with Katharine as she slept that next morning when he appeared in the doorway and asked me to step out into the hall. By the look on his face, I knew the news was bad. He explained that tests showed Katharine had metastatic lung cancer that had spread to her brain, to her bones, and to other parts of her body. He said that she had about two months left to live. He recommended that I take her home where she could be cared for by family and hospice nurses. With that news, the walls and the ceiling seemed to come crashing down around me.

Katharine had been a heavy smoker all of her adult life. Nothing that I or the children or her doctor said could persuade her to give up cigarettes. Then one morning I saw an ad in the newspaper about a hypnotist in Ottawa, Illinois, who claimed he had a 90 percent success rate getting heavy smokers to give up smoking. I was excited to learn this and immediately told Katharine about him and asked if she would see him. She agreed to go. I even took my sister Laura Jane, another heavy smoker, with us.

Laura Jane's first session with the hypnotist was successful, and she has never smoked another cigarette since. However, Katharine was lighting up a cigarette just as soon as she walked out of the building. I don't think she was ever serious about trying to stop smoking.

On the morning of Wednesday, May 9, 2007, she died peacefully at home surrounded by our family and two hospice nurses. With her death, that pattern of good following bad that I had been experiencing for decades ended. The truth is that nothing good has happened to me since her death.

Family and friends help us tremendously at times like this, but grief, I learned, is something we have to go through alone, in our own way and at our own pace. At an early age, I learned something about stoicism that has stayed with me. When I lost Katharine, I lost way more than a wife and a mother to my children. She did a great job with our kids. So much responsibility fell on her shoulders, especially because I was gone so much of the time the kids were growing up. She took an interest in my job, like no other coach's wife I know of. She read magazines and coaches' manuals, and stayed up with the game so that she was able to make suggestions to me that helped me grow in my role as coach. She was sometimes like my assistant coach. She entertained our recruits and their parents; she went on all of my clinic trips all over the world. She attended meetings and made friends with other coaches and their wives. She held an annual Kentucky Invitational Tournament open house, often with nearly a hundred guests. She was my partner in every way, the ideal coach's wife.

She did not like the stress of the games. As you know, Wildcat fans can get awfully demanding at times. During close games, Katharine walked the halls rather than listen or watch. The pressure that comes with winning or losing was too hard on her.

After her death, I got by slowly with good help. Judy Coffey, who worked for us the last five years of Katharine's life, still comes three times a week to clean, and I greatly appreciate her help. I have learned to do a few things around the house for myself, things that I should have learned years ago, such as using the washer and dryer, and also the dishwasher.

The microwave is handy. Plus I have learned to cook a few things, a very few things, that will go together in one pot on the stove. I don't like to make messes that I have to clean up. One-pot recipes are the best for me, but I can cook a good steak and a baked potato. Fortunately, my friends and family often invite me to dine with them. I fix my own breakfast and have it alone at home. Then I enjoy going out to lunch almost daily with some of my old buddies, former players, and businessmen interested in Wildcat activities at the little ROC Cafe attached to the nearby Immanuel Baptist Church on Tates Creek Road. It is a good group to be with, and no matter who shows up, we always have fun being together. A recent friend is Clint Griffith, who amazes me and others with his unique ability to repair large and small appliances that the rest of us would just throw away.

37

My Thank-You Note

When I think back to my childhood, and I often do, I think about my parents, who instilled in me the virtues and understanding of what is necessary for a purposeful life. They were great role models. Both were honest, hardworking, intelligent people, respected in their community. They had many good friends. I learned the value of friendship early on. I watched their successes as I grew older. I understood why they disciplined me and kept me from making decisions that may have led to bad consequences.

I have learned that self-satisfaction with a job well done means more than trophies or awards. Even when I was a young boy, after working long days in the field, I enjoyed standing on a hill and looking back at the sticks of tobacco I had cut, row after row, or seeing a field of shocked corn that I had put up that day. I could see my accomplishments, and it was a great feeling. It was a feeling of being a contributor to this good earth. Those experiences of feeling a job well done I carried over to every endeavor or challenge that I faced. My success was a feeling of personal gratification. What success I had in coaching was never my individual effort alone; it was a shared success with my boys and all my assistants, as well as our supporters.

The friends I had growing up were and still are important to me. They are Richard Wilson, Billy Fitzgerald, Paul Hicks, Cavin Barnett, John Swinford, Lewis and Steamboat Tolle, Goo Goo, and June Bug.

My assistant coaches were the finest young men, and without them I could not have done what I did. They were all hardworking, loyal, and intelligent, and they all had a passion for basketball.

Boyd Grant. The second assistant coach I hired was Boyd Grant from Colorado State, where he had worked with head coach Jim Williams, renowned in the West. I got to know and respect Boyd for his coaching abilities while we were both coaching in the Rocky Mountains. That's while I was at Regis. He was a great defensive coach. I turned the defensive drill teaching over to him. He was also a great recruiter and judge of talent. He was the lead recruiter for Mike Phillips.

Jim Hatfield. I hired Jim when I had an opening after Boyd took a coaching job at Southern Idaho. Jim was the lead recruiter for Rick Robey in Louisiana. He organized Rick's letter signing at the famous Antoine's restaurant in New Orleans, celebrating by arranging a basketball-shaped baked Alaska for dessert. Jim had great knowledge of the game. He was successful as head coach at Southwest Louisiana, at Mississippi State, and at Hardin-Simmons.

Leonard Hamilton. I was very lucky to be looking for an assistant when Lake Kelly resigned from Austin Peay and recommended his assistant, Leonard Hamilton, to me. I knew Leonard as a "bird dog" recruiter who recruited "Fly" Williams to Austin Peay. My first meeting with Leonard was after we had beaten Austin Peay in the first round of the Mid East Regionals in 1973. I was walking down the hall, and as I passed him he said to me in a very upbeat manner, "Congratulations, Coach, but we'll get you the next time." I liked his enthusiasm and his love for recruiting. He did a super job of loading our roster to make my job easier. He is one of the best defensive coaches in the game today. He has had success in both the college and the pro game.

Leonard is a great person and fun to be with. We had many memorable recruiting trips together. But I'll always remember the time we visited a recruit in Newark, New Jersey. We flew into Newark and rented a car to drive to the place where the game was being held. At this time, of course, there was no internet, no Google Maps. Unfortunately, Leonard had no sense of direction—and he was driving. We kept ending up, no matter which road we took, on the edge of a cliff or on a dead-end street overlooking the very interstate that we should have been on. Leonard would say, "Coach, we should be down there." I'd say, "Okay, let's see how we can get down there." Eventually we did get to our destination, albeit late.

Another thing about Leonard and rental cars: he always had to call Hertz or Avis to send him his briefcase or piece of luggage that he had left in the car. I should have known he had this habit when on his first visit to UK he locked his keys in his car. But the fact is, when it came to coaching basketball, he knew right down to the smallest detail what to teach or do.

Lynn Nance. I met Lynn (six foot five) when he was investigating for the NCAA. A former FBI agent, he had come to UK to check on our compliance. I was impressed with him from the first time I met him. He was very professional and thorough. Before he left after our interview, he asked me if I knew of anyone who was looking for an assistant. I told him I didn't know of any opening, but if I heard of anything, I'd let him know. Later on, when I had a position open up, I remembered his inquiry, and he welcomed the opportunity to work with us.

Lynn's NCAA experience was most valuable in so many ways, especially in recruiting. I told him to carefully check all recruiting rules before we had a high school player come in for a visit. We always cleared all activities with Lynn. When I told him I was taking a recruit to Claiborne Farm for a tour, he questioned whether or not it was legal, since the destination was outside of Fayette County. I asked him to check with the chief rule's interpreter, Bob McMenamin. After Lynn explained how many horse farms there are in the area, Bob approved the trip on the grounds that Claiborne was a part of the continuous environment. Later, during an NCAA hearing about those tours, Bob McMenamin said he couldn't remember Lynn's phone call and that we should have gotten the approval in writing. The NCAA charged us with five violations for taking recruits to Claiborne.

Lynn left us to take the head coaching job at Iowa State. From there, he went on to Central Missouri, where I had coached. He won a Division II NCAA National Championship.

Joe Dean. Joe is the son of Joe (String Music) Dean Sr., who was a PR leader and sales manager for Converse and later athletic director at LSU. Joe Jr. was a tough player and competitor at Mississippi State. His aggressive personality caught my attention, so when I needed a graduate assistant, I brought him onboard. I later moved him up to full-time assistant when Dick Parsons left.

Dick Parsons. A good floor coach, Dick kept his cool and kept me out of trouble. I would feel his tug on my coat tail whenever I was too aggressive going after a referee. Dick resigned from our staff after the NCAA ruled that only full-time coaches could go on the road to recruit. The ruling forced him to decide either to go on the road more to recruit and do less floor coaching or declassify to part-time assistant and stay in the house. He did not like either option and so he resigned.

Dick and I enjoyed fishing together. One time, while we were fishing in Townsend Creek, we split up: I went downstream to fish the rapids and chug holes, and Dick went upstream to fish the dead water. Later, when we got back to the truck, I had a beautiful string of smallmouth and red eye, approximately twenty keepers. Dick had the cooler up on the truck. I asked him how he had done. He said, "Not as good as you, but I got a few nice ones." I opened the cooler and there were three largemouth bass totaling fourteen pounds.

The players went to Dick for consolation after I had given them a good tongue lashing. He was good working with the boys. He recruited several important players, too, including Larry Johnson, Freddie Cowan, and Dwane Casey.

Jim Long. As a graduate assistant, Jim joined my staff in 1976 on a part-time basis as junior varsity coach and scout.

Bill Keightley. Bill was our manager and a lot more. He was truly a father figure for the players, who often came to him for comfort and advice. He was a great guy and a strong supporter of our program. He earned the name Mr. Wildcat! Everybody loved Bill.

Walt McCombs. Walt, our trainer, was by far better at his job than anyone else I have ever met. He, too, was a friend to the players and to me and my assistants.

Adding so much to my long good life is my family. I have been blessed with good children and grandchildren. I give great credit for them to my wife. When the children were growing up, I had to be away from home so many times, and she was left alone with the responsibility of being both mother and father. In addition, she had the responsibilities of keeping our house. She did a tremendous job, too. She was a beautiful, kind, and gracious person. I am grateful for having had Katharine in my life.

Also, I am proud of our three children. Judy, our oldest, is a CPA and married to Rick Derrickson, who is a retired postmaster. Kathy is a retired nurse, and she is married to Mike Summers, assistant football coach at the University of Louisville. Steve is our horse farm manager and vice president of collections at Central Bank. I have three grandchildren: Jeff Derrickson and his wife Kelly are the owners of Tropical Smoothie Restaurant in Lexington. Laura Derrickson is a speech therapist employed by the Columbus, Ohio, public school system. Amy Summers Lawyer is finishing her doctorate in equine science and leadership at the University of Kentucky, where she also teaches. She and her husband Ben have two sons, Joe Brack and Tyson—my great-grandsons.

I couldn't finish this book without mentioning my fond memories of my friends at Shepherdsville, at Regis, and at Central Missouri. At UK, I had developed many long-lasting friends who helped keep UK basketball on top. All of them were among my closest friends and still are today. Of course, my brother Billy Hall tops the list. I still miss running things by him today.

Part of that huge village I talked about earlier are what I call my outdoor friends. Terry McBrayer is the best outdoorsman ever in hunting, fishing, and camping. Bob Maxwell and Carl Hamilton are present-day Daniel Boones. Russell Rice was a great fishing buddy. Joe Kendall could fix anything; he could repair motors and do all kinds of electrical work, a jack of all trades. Brown Badgett loved the outdoors as much as I do and was a great and generous friend. More than just an assistant, Dick Parsons was a good companion. One time Dick and I attempted a four-way day: rising before daylight to hunt squirrels, catch a limit of bass, shoot a limit of doves, and after dark get a limit of frogs. To know the outcome, you will have to check with Dick because I was too tired to count that night after we came in.

Big-time helpers were Seth Hancock who went to Germany with me to help recruit. I owe huge thanks to Don Webb and Dudley Webb, who helped me with every project I attempted. They are great men, community leaders. I am also grateful to Van Florence and the 101 Members, the best support group a coach could have.

Cecil Dunn came to my office as a law student and helped me with recruiting. Don Johnson, Rod Hatfield, Paul Miller, Elmer Whitaker, Luther Deaton, Cap Hershey, Ed Niebert, and Richard Maloney all helped with getting summer jobs for the players and often with making private airplanes available for recruiting. Oscar Combs, with his publications of the *Cats Pause*, did so much to create fan support for the Wildcats and did wonders in building the Big Blue Nation. Also, Roy Holsclaw, Jim Rhodes, Bob Atkins, and L. D. Gorman. Joe Gentry and Dave Drake are always there when I need them. They contributed largely to building the lodge and Rupp Arena. All these men have helped me throughout the years in many ways.

My secretary, Marta McMackin, was a patient, wonderful, intelligent woman who did so many things for me and our basketball program. I will never forget her.

Jim Lankster remains a close friend today, although I don't get to see him as often as I'd like since we both retired from the radio station. He and his wife Flo love traveling abroad, and do so often. A loyal friend, Jim served me in several capacities. He was my assistant coach in 1979–1980. When the NCAA made us make changes in our new lodge and also had us move some regular students into the residence, Jim was there to help. We wrote letters to high school principals telling them our needs and asking them to recommend good students whom they thought would fit in well with our athletes and inspire study and classroom success. Jim helped select those boys who moved in with our players and got along with them so well. After Coach Dean left, Jim was in charge of organizing and setting up the summer camps. Also, after my friend and radio program manager Dick Robinson died, Jim became the producer of the *Joe B. and Denny Show*. He was often my driver, secretary, schedule-keeper, and loyal companion. And he is a chef! Jim loves to cook, especially fish dishes, and I have enjoyed many wonderful meals with him and Flo in their home.

I appreciate that my hometown, Cynthiana, Kentucky, had a mural of me painted on one of its downtown buildings. The artist, Sergio Odeith, did a wonderful job. I thank him.

When some of the University of Kentucky administrators approached me about building a new Wildcat Lodge, they said they did not want to hurt my feelings by tearing the old one down. I told them no, I would not be upset. Quite the contrary, I was happy to know that the old one would be replaced with a new and better facility. The old lodge had served its purpose well for a number of years, but it needed to be replaced. I assured them that I would be delighted if a new lodge was built for the boys. Then they also told me they were going to honor me with a statue as a way of commemorating my raising the money and building the first Wildcat Lodge. I told them I never wanted a statue, that it was not necessary for the university to provide any more places for pigeons to rest—which is all a statue of me would be, a restroom station for birds. I just did not like the idea of seeing an image of myself standing on a pedestal somewhere on the campus—even if Coach Calipari did say he would clean my statue every day.

Nonetheless, when they built the beautiful Wildcat Coal

Lodge, they commissioned an artist to create the statue near the entrance. When I saw it for the first time at its dedication, I was astonished and delighted to see my likeness the way the sculptor had created it. I was depicted in a four-hundred-pound bronze statue seated on an iron bench, with room for two others on the bench with me. The sculptor did a fantastic job. He placed me sitting in a coaching stance, leaning forward with anticipation, holding my rolled-up program in my right hand as I always did. In the end I was glad they insisted on a statue. What an honor! I thank J. Brett Grill, the sculptor, for the natural manner in which he portrayed me. (I even forgot about his neglecting to make me look like Cary Grant as I had requested.) At the dedication, I shook hands with him and thanked him. And I thank him here again now. I really like that statue! I enjoy it, too, when co-eds come sit by me and have their pictures taken with me.

Finally, I pay tribute to all the coaches who followed me, especially to Coach John Calipari. I thank him for making me feel appreciated. I am thrilled to get calls from him telling me news or about some upcoming event. Cal is a gentleman and a great coach. He knows how to teach the present-day game. He is not only a master recruiter, he also has a gift for marketing our program in innovating ways that attract fans to the Kentucky Wildcats and our Big Blue Nation. I wish the best for him and hope he remains our coach for many years.

Now, as I come to the close of this long narrative, I worry that I may have left out some of you who have befriended me. Please forgive me and attribute this omission to the mind-bleep of a very old codger. You will definitely be in my next book!

Acknowledgments

For years after I retired, my family and a few close friends kept telling me that I ought to write a book. The older I got, the more they urged me to record my experiences. My children even gave me a recorder, but I did not like sitting alone talking to a machine. Many excellent sportswriters, too, offered to write a book about me. The problem was I did not know what kind of book I wanted. I only knew for certain that I did not want a typical basketball book.

Then, one day years ago, my friend Jim Lankster handed me a small book with a strange title: *When Cuba Conquered Kentucky*, by Marianne Walker, and told me to read it. He said, "It's about that little team that won the state championship in 1952, but it is also about much more than basketball. If you like it, then this writer may be someone you might want to talk to someday."

I read that book and loved it. It is one of my favorite books. In writing about the Cuba Cubs, Marianne told where those boys came from, how they lived, and how their coach lived. She described little Cuba, Kentucky, and told how its people supported its team. Her words painted pictures. I could see it all as I read. She wrote so much more than a basketball book. That was the kind of book I wanted about my life. I wanted what I call a friendly-written book about my life before and after I became a coach. I wanted it written so my grandchildren and family that followed as well as others interested would know what my life was like before I became the coach of a very famous team. I believed Marianne Walker would be the one to help me tell my story.

I first met her after Jim Lankster, our radio program manager, and I invited her to be on our radio program to talk about *When*

Cuba Conquered Kentucky. We invited her again in 2013 when the new edition of that book came out, retitled *The Graves County Boys.* Also, she and her husband were with me on a couple of other occasions. I liked her personality, and I liked the way she writes.

Working with her on this project has been a good experience, and I agree with her belief that it is always healthy to have a goal to work toward. Because of Marianne's encouragement, expertise, talent and, yes, patience, I now have "my book" the way I always wanted it. I am thankful for her help.

Joe B. Hall

I will always be grateful to Coach Hall for recruiting me to go along with him on this road trip, for sharing his memories with me and now with you. This is Joe B. Hall's story—his life as he wants to tell it, as he wants it known to his family, friends, sports fans, and all who remember him and an unforgettable era of basketball in the Commonwealth of Kentucky.

Many people contributed to this book. Jim Lankster took pictures for the book, brought me together with key people, generously shared his own experiences working with Coach Hall, and assisted in other ways too numerous to mention.

Mrs. Huda Jones graciously opened her home in Lexington to my husband Ulvester and me when we traveled to Lexington to work with Coach Hall.

Kentucky Wildcats Jim Andrews, Kyle Macy, Larry Stamper, Jerry Hale, Jack Givens, and Louie Dampier shared some of their essential and much-appreciated memories.

Roy Holsclaw, a founding member of the Alley Cats, explained the vital role that he and that group played in supporting the UK athletic program and in building Rupp Arena and the first Wildcat Lodge.

Jeff Douglas, the director of the library at Knox College in Galesburg, Illinois, gets my heartfelt thanks. He is a dear friend of many years to whom I have often turned with questions about research and writing.

Thomas Jones, my son-in-law and our family's enthusiastic basketball authority, gave me good questions to ask about games. I also appreciate the help I always get from Retta Zollinger and the other employees at our great Henderson County Public Library.

I am grateful to Pratt Lewis for speaking to me about Sewanee.

Ulvester Walker, my husband, stood beside me with his love and support throughout this project, as he always has in all I have ever done. He patiently double-checked for me more scores, spellings, dates, and drafts than I care to count.

Marianne Walker

Index

Index

Index

Index

Victory Gardens, 26
Vitale, Dick, 168

Wachs, Fred, 151, 152
Walker, Cozel, 98–99
Walker, Kenny, 100, 166–67
Wallace, Perry, 99
Ward, Bob, 52
Warford, Reggie, 100
Webb, Don, 149–50
Webb, Dudley, 149–50
Western Kentucky University, 116
Westwood One Radio, 170, 171
Wildcat Foundation, Inc., 150
Wildcat Lodge, 149–51, 153–58

Wilkins, Dominique, x
Williams, LaVon, 100, 141, 162
Williams, Roy, ix
Wilson, Earl, 168
Wooden, John, ix, x, 104, 137–40,
  168–69
Woodward, Bob, 138
World Tour, US State Department
  (1951), 56–60
World War II, 25–26

Xavier University, 51

Yessin, Humsey, 32, 33, 35